THE WALDHEIM FILES

THE
WALDHEIM FILES
Myth and Reality

MICHAEL PALUMBO

faber and faber

LONDON · BOSTON

First published in 1988
by Faber and Faber Limited
3 Queen Square London WC1N 3AU

Photoset by Parker Typesetting Service Leicester
Printed in Great Britain by
Richard Clay Ltd Bungay Suffolk

British Library Cataloguing in Publication Data

Palumbo, Michael
The Waldheim files: myth and reality.
1. Waldheim, Kurt   2. World War,
1939–1945 – Campaigns – Balkan Peninsula
I. Title
940.54'21   D766
ISBN 0-571-15087-X

To Alan Chazanow

Contents

List of illustrations

List of abbreviations for document collections and archival sources

Acknowledgements

Thanks are in order to the staffs of the Public Record Office in London and the United States National Archives and the Washington National Record Center. Particular help was extended by Alf Erlardson and his staff at the UN Archives. Valuable information was also obtained from the World Jewish Congress, the Austrian Press and Information Service, Kurt Waldheim's lawyers, the Justice Department's Office of Special Investigation and various sources in the United Nations and Yugoslavia. Unfortunately, I found myself compelled to come to conclusions which will probably displease all of the participants in this controversy who provide me with information.

Julian O'Halloran and his producer, Indra de Lanerolle, at BBC *Newsnight* proved to be stimulating colleagues while working on the Waldheim story. Keith Hindell of BBC has been helpful both in 1980 and during the preparation of this book.

Useful advice on literary matters was obtained from Joel Agee while Ilan Hazout helped with translations from Hebrew. The greatest assistance was given by Alan Chazanow who made his impressive collection of materials on war crimes available to me. It is to him that this book is gratefully dedicated.

Foreword

For the past two years the American and European press have carried numerous articles about the Kurt Waldheim affair. Almost all these stories, which concentrate on the former UN Secretary General's Wehrmacht career, paint a picture of a man who hid his Balkan military service because of war crimes. Waldheim has become a symbol of the Nazi era. In America he is useful to the powerful Zionist lobby not only in exposing Austria's Nazi past but, more important, in discrediting the UN – which made many anti-Israeli resolutions while Waldheim was Secetary General, including the 1975 declaration equating Zionism with racism. To the French and Dutch, Waldheim evokes memories of the bitter Nazi occupation, while in Italy the left sees him as the conservative president of Austria – the traditional enemy. Even in Germany, many are keen to condemn Waldheim as a war criminal and this is made easier because he is not a German. And of course in Yugoslavia Waldheim provides a convenient opportunity to publicize the Nazi atrocities of the Second World War. Britain remains one of the few countries where an unemotional discussion of the Waldheim affair is possible.

The press in all countries has succumbed to the 'cutting file' mentality. The practice has been to write stories with headlines based on 'new revelations' by one of Waldheim's more irresponsible critics while the body of the article includes a rehash of long-standing allegations. Invariably missing is any documentation showing that Waldheim actually ordered or was in any way criminally responsible for atrocities.

In reality, while almost all the attention has been focused

on the former UN Secretary General's 'Nazi past', the Waldheim affair is not primarily a war crimes case but a story of Cold War attempts at blackmail, and international intrigue. Although Waldheim is not guilty of atrocities, there is evidence to suggest that the former UN Secretary General *is* guilty of being influenced by those who knew about his false war crimes file. It should be noted that the Waldheim story was first presented to the press by the World Jewish Congress (WJC) which received considerable support from the American Zionists who sought to discredit the UN. It obviously served their purposes to claim that the UN was headed by a former Nazi war criminal rather than explore the complex story of his post-war intelligence contacts with several countries, including Israel.

Despite evidence to the contrary, the press has perpetuated the myth that the Waldheim case is about Nazi atrocities. Many newspaper editors have a 'don't confuse the public with the facts' attitude, even though all serious researchers working on the Waldheim case (including the former historical consultant to the WJC) now accept that the original UN War Crimes Commission charges were brought against him in 1948 by the Yugoslavs for political reasons and not because he was a war criminal. Some claim to have discovered evidence that the Yugoslavs 'framed the right man', implying that though Waldheim's 1948 UN war crimes file is patently bogus, they have recently discovered real evidence against him – but the documents presented fall far short of making any case. Because of the complexity of this story, there is a need for a serious examination of the facts.

Based on extensive archival research, interviews both on and off the record, and my own experiences since 1979, I have worked for two years to put together the following pieces of the Waldheim puzzle.

1. Although he denies it, in his student days in the late 1930s Kurt Waldheim joined the Nazi student union and a Nazi-sponsored riding club. Membership in these organizations was practically compulsory and did not indicate any ideological preference particularly since Waldheim never joined the Nazi party itself.

2. During the war Waldheim was wounded on the Russian front, after which he was sent to the Balkans as a staff officer, performing largely clerical functions. He had neither command powers nor the opportunity to commit war crimes. However, during the latter part of the war he served as an intelligence officer on an army group staff where he learned a great deal about the Communist partisans who would come to rule Yugoslavia.

3. In 1945 Waldheim surrendered to the Americans, who clearly appreciated his fund of information about Communist Yugoslavia. He was hired by the Vienna Foreign Office – a centre of Western influence in a country and government divided by the British, French, Americans and Russians. Waldheim worked as an aide to Foreign Minister Karl Gruber, a man with close links to US intelligence.

4. In an effort to embarrass Gruber, Soviet and Yugoslav intelligence fabricated a phoney UN War Crimes Commission file against Waldheim. The plan was to create a scandal by forcing Waldheim to resign but at the last minute the plan was cancelled since Waldheim was transferred to the Austrian embassy in Paris.

5. Waldheim claims that after 1949 the Yugoslavs forgot about him and his war crimes file, but there is evidence to the contrary. Waldheim began to conceal his military service in the Balkans not because he was a war criminal but because he feared the false war crimes file and other documents held by the Yugoslavs.

6. There is evidence that Waldheim was caught up in the complex intrigue involving British, American, Soviet and Yugoslav intelligence agencies that characterized post-war Vienna. His loyalty is not clear but he probably favoured the West.

7. In the 1971 era of *détente* Waldheim was the ideal candidate for UN Secretary General since both the Soviets and Americans had access to his war crimes file which, though fake, was embarrassing enough to force the 'conscience of mankind' to resign. Throughout Waldheim's term as Secretary General rumours about him circulated in New York and Vienna.

8. As Secretary General, Waldheim served the interests of the superpowers, who appointed him against the Third World countries who sought to end US and USSR domination of the UN. The Austrian diplomat was also very considerate of Israel and Yugoslavia, countries which had access to information on his hidden past.

9. In 1979 I discovered that the records of the UN War Crimes Commission were being secretly held in the UN archives but I was unable to gain access. Shortly afterwards the US Justice Department obtained the register of the names of all those listed with the UN War Crimes Commission. The Justice Department made no move at this time against Waldheim, who was on the list but still being protected by the CIA while he remained Secretary General. The Justice Department probably realized that Waldheim's war crimes file was a fake.

10. In March 1986, shortly after Waldheim announced his campaign for the presidency of Austria, the WJC publicized Waldheim's war-time service in the Balkans and his war crimes file. The WJC apparently acted against the wishes of the CIA and the government of Israel, which was already aware of the file.

11. In May 1987, under pressure from the American Zionist lobby, the Justice Department put Waldheim on its 'watch list' of those barred from entry into the US, based on a report kept secret because of its lack of any incriminating documentation.

The story of Kurt Waldheim is not a pleasant one. There are no heroes. There is, in fact, more than enough blame to be shared in generous amounts by the US Justice Department, the World Jewish Congress, the intelligence services of various nations, the press in too many countries to mention, the United Nations and, not least, Waldheim himself – a man whose love of public office and attention is at the heart of the enigma.

Michael Palumbo
New York
February 1988

Prologue

'You're from the Secretariat, aren't you?' the young woman behind the desk asked. Realizing that I was likely to get better service in the United Nations library if they thought I was an employee of the UN, I answered in the affirmative. 'Where can I find the files of the UN War Crimes Commission,' I inquired. Although on that autumn day in 1979 there were no indications where the files were kept, my common sense told me that the UNWCC files which I needed to complete a book must be somewhere in the UN, despite the fact that there was no mention of these records in the UN library card catalogue.

'Perhaps those files are in the UN archives,' the young librarian responded. Like most historians in 1979, I had never heard of the UN archives. A few moments later the librarian presented me with the index to 'record group 30'. It was marked 'Confidential' and listed all the war crimes files held by the UN. It didn't take long to realize that I had made an important discovery.

For some time I had been working on a book about Fascist Italy in the Second World War. In my research (I have a Ph.D in history) I had uncovered considerable evidence of massive Italian Fascist atrocities including concentration camps, the use of poison gas and plans to eliminate entire ethnic groups in Africa and the Balkans. I had also found indications of an Anglo-American cover-up of Italian Fascist war crimes after the Second World War.[1] There were references in several

1. My work was featured in an article that appeared in *Epoca* on 17 January 1988 entitled 'Genocidio All'Italiana'. This story was carried by every major newspaper in Italy.

sources to a United Nations War Crimes Commission but no indication as to where the files might be located. No author writing on Axis war crimes had ever located these files but I was determined to find them. My hunch that the files must be somewhere at the UN paid off.

The day after my discovery of the index I visited the UN archives. With me was James F. Demos, a friend who served as director of the Hellenic Freedom Foundation. James had immediately recognized the importance of my discovery and was eager to help, particularly since many Greeks had been killed by the Axis forces in the Second World War.

The UN archives were located on the eleventh and twelfth floors of an office building on Park Avenue South. As we walked into the building my suspicions were aroused by the lack of any indication in the directory in the lobby that the UN archives were located in the building. James and I soon met Alf Erlandson, the chief archivist, who was obviously in a delicate position as official keeper of the UNWCC files.

Erlandson gave some feeble excuses as to why the UNWCC records were kept secret. He said that the files contained only the names of minor suspects since all the 'big fish' had been tried after the war. He seemed embarrassed and anxious to prove that he was not part of any cover-up. He made it clear that a large part of the UNWCC files were open, including the proceedings of the various committees of the Commission. But the material giving the charges and evidence against the 40,000 suspected war criminals was strictly confidential. James and I indicated to Erlandson our sustained interest in the files and our desire to change the status of the records so that they could be made available to war crimes investigators.

In the following weeks James checked his political contacts in Washington to see who might be interested in helping us gain access to the files. Meanwhile I continued to visit the archives, where I examined the open portion of the UNWCC records and spoke with Erlandson. He told me some remarkable things. Over the years no other scholar had asked about the files except an eccentric Dutchman who was interested in Japanese war criminals. Erlandson showed me a letter from the man, who was clearly demented. Other private individuals who had made inquiries to the UN information service were told that the files were not at the UN. Erlandson said that this was the policy of the previous chief archivist, which he had changed when he found out about it.

After I had gained his confidence, Erlandson took me downstairs to see the files. I could not believe that the security was so lax. The files were protected by a screen door. Its lock could have been picked by any fifteen-year-old street criminal armed with a safety pin.

'Let's take a look at one,' Erlandson said as he picked out a dossier at random from a box containing the files of Germans who had committed crimes in Yugoslavia (he would not let me glance at any of the records of Italians who had committed crimes in Yugoslavia since he feared I would recognize the names). I noticed that the dossiers listed evidence against each suspect. It was clear that Erlandson did not fully appreciate the importance of the UNWCC files or he would never have allowed me to see so much. In any case, since I indicated to him that there might be publicity on this question, he was anxious to appear on the side of the angels.

During this period Erlandson allowed me to look at the UN correspondence relating to the UNWCC files. I found that the original policy of the War Crimes Commission had been to make the files available 'upon official written request of a member state of the United Nations'. This rule had been approved by both Lord Wright, the chairman of the Commission, and Dr J. J. Litawski, its legal officer. But in 1949 UN officials had changed the rules without consulting Lord

Wright or Dr Litawski. The new rule determined that the sensitive portions of the files 'may be inspected and used only for official United Nations purposes'. Dr Ivan Kerno, the assistant Secretary General for legal affairs who changed the rules, based his decision on a number of highly questionable assumptions. In a memorandum of 2 November 1949 Kerno stated that it had not been the policy of the War Crimes Commission to make its documents available to member governments: but making its documents available to enable member governments to pursue and prosecute war criminals was the very purpose of the UNWCC. The 1980 policy had the effect of denying the use of these files to member governments which were attempting to carry out the original intentions of the War Crimes Commission.

Dr Kerno stated in his memorandum that 'this material had not been submitted to judicial process or otherwise subjected to legal evaluation'.[1] This is true since the files do contain extremely raw data but there is no reason why this information should not be used by legitimate war crimes investigators. Indeed, it was entirely proper to make the files available to member governments, since it would enable them to act in conformity with UN policy as established by the General Assembly, whose resolution 3(I), of 13 February 1946, on the 'Extradition and Punishment of War Criminals' recommended that governments do all in their power to pursue war criminals.

By preventing member governments from using the UNWCC files the UN was discouraging member states from carrying out not only the original intention of the War Crimes Commission but the will of the General Assembly. This was particularly noticeable in relation to the UNWCC's list of the

1. UNA Central Registry File, memorandum by Ivan Kerno, 2 November 1949.

names of the 40,000 suspects, which the Commission had declassified in December 1946. This list should have been kept with the non-restricted portion of the UNWCC files together with the committee proceedings but the UN had placed it with the restricted materials. As I examined the UN correspondence I noticed that this list was so secret that when several governments had made inquiries in the 1950s, the UN had refused to confirm or deny who was on this list. Up to 1980 the only time the files were made available was for the Eichmann trial in Israel in 1960.

The UNWCC had been formed during the war to punish Axis war criminals. Its principal function was to evaluate evidence on particular suspected war criminals and report to member governments when there was sufficient evidence for a prima facie case against an individual. With the help of national offices established by many countries betweeen 1944 and 1948, cases were developed against about 40,000 Axis war criminals. The UNWCC did not apprehend or prosecute war criminals. The theory was, however, that if people were listed as war criminals by the UNWCC, it would be easier for the country where the crimes took place to extradite a suspect from his native country or a country where he might be hiding.

In 1949 the UNWCC went out of business. Because of Cold War tension, the British and Americans began to view Axis war criminals as potential allies against the Soviet Union. The Russians had never joined the UNWCC so that the Western Allies who had controlled the Commission decided to turn its files of unprosecuted suspects over to the UN. All seventeen members of the UNWCC kept numerous copies of the list of 40,000 suspects – which included Kurt Waldheim's name.

I was particularly concerned that the files be made available to the Justice Department, which was then supposedly seeking to deport Nazi and Eastern European war criminals who had entered the USA after the Second World War. Some of these people had been brought to the USA by the Central Intelligence Agency (CIA), wishing to use their technical and military information. In response to congressional pressure under the Carter administration, the Justice Department had set up an Office of Special Investigations (OSI) to seek the deportation of Nazi war criminals. But the Department's zeal in pursuing this goal was not greatly in evidence. I was not surprised when Erlandson told me that the Justice Department had inquired about the UNWCC files on several occasions but the OSI had never followed through.

I did not trust the US mission to the United Nations, since I suspected that the State Department, like the CIA, was probably involved in the cover-up of Nazi war criminals. James Demos and I decided instead to take our case to members of Congress who might be interested. First we wanted to visit a few of the UN missions most concerned with this subject. Our list included most of the members of the original War Crimes Commission (France, Czechoslovakia, Poland, Greece, Yugoslavia, Ethiopia) plus, for obvious reasons, Israel and West Germany. The reaction of each government was most instructive and interesting.

Because of James Demos's connections, we first went to the Greek UN mission, where we expected and received considerate attention. Before our visit, Ambassador Katapodis had inquired with the UN legal office and been denied access to the restricted portions of the UNWCC files. The ambassador told us that these files were not a minor issue but an 'important question which could lead to serious international repercussions'. According to him the decision to keep the files closed involved 'the highest levels of the United Nations'. The Greek ambassador indicated his belief that in 1949 the US State Department, with the possible agreement of the USSR, had informed the Secretary General that the UNWCC files should not be available for further war crime trials. The ambassador was very cordial and diplomatic, but he clearly wanted us to know that we might have bitten off more than we could chew.

The next day we visited the West German mission to the UN, where we spoke to Minister-Counsellor Dr Hans-Joachim Vergau. When we told him of our plan to try to change the status of record group 30, he expressed a desire that the matter not become a 'Cold War issue'. He denied that there had been a cover-up of the UNWCC records and said that his government preferred that the matter be treated as a 'legal and bureaucratic' rather than a 'political or human rights issue'. I was not surprised by his attitude, but I was taken aback by his candour.

At the French UN mission, the legal counsellor expressed relief when I assured him that there were no dossiers on French collaborators in the UNWCC files. But he was apprehensive about the possible reaction of the French left to the news of the war crimes files cover-up. When I asked what attitude the French government would take on the opening of the UNWCC files, the counsellor indicated that it was a sensitive subject which could affect the economic, political and diplomatic relations between France and West Germany. He added, 'As an historian you must realize that relations between France and Germany are always a delicate matter which must be handled with care.' It was clear to me that France wanted the UN war crimes files kept secret.[1]

Our next meeting was at the Yugoslav UN mission. When James Demos had called to make the appointment, the Yugoslavs had asked him many questions, so that they had a good

---

1. In the 1970s France had obtained a copy of Waldheim's war record from the Austrian archives. See Chapter V.

idea of the situation before we arrived. Shortly after entering the mission, we were taken to a dimly lit room with a decor that seemed East European antique. We were met by two diplomats who conducted the interview almost in the manner of an interrogation; politely, but with a *modus operandi* which might have been taken from Kafka. One man asked questions while the other wrote down my answers. 'Why have you come here?' 'Who else have you contacted?' 'Are you looking for evidence about a particular person?' 'What is your ultimate goal with regard to record group 30?' I naturally chose my answers to these questions carefully.

The Yugoslavs seemed pleased when I told them that in the 1940s, when the UNWCC was in operation, Yugoslavia had rigorously opposed the Anglo-American effort to shield the Axis war criminals. I told them that I was confident that Yugoslavia was not involved in any present effort to cover up the UNWCC files. They promised to discuss the matter with the UN legal office and to make a full report on the files of their ministry in Belgrade. They also promised to look into the war crimes files held by Yugoslavia. I was happy that Yugoslavia was taking the matter so seriously, but I could not understand why they were so interested.

It was now time to go to Congress to present our case to members of the House and Senate. As mentioned, we did not trust the US mission to the UN. In 1960 the then ambassador to the UN, Henry Cabot Lodge, had stated in a Security Council debate on Adolf Eichmann that 'in lists submitted to the United Nations War Crimes Commission Eichmann was described as a war criminal by at least three of the countries which suffered under Hitler. I refer to France, Czechoslovakia and the Netherlands.' Cabot Lodge could not have known about this unless he had access to the list of those named in the UNWCC records. UN policy at this time was neither to confirm nor deny that anyone was on the UNWCC list. Thus the US government had copies of the UNWCC list of war criminals which included Adolf Eichmann, as well as Kurt Waldheim.[1]

Many members of Congress were already suspicious of the State Department because it had aided the CIA in bringing Nazis into the USA after the Second World War. James Demos called Senator Max Bacus, who headed a committee which had uncovered Nazis in the USA. Senator Bacus put us in contact with Franklin Silby, an aide who had conducted numerous investigations of war criminals. We also contacted Congressman Lester Wolfe, whom James had known for many years.

On 25 February 1980 we visited Washington, where we spoke to both Silby and Wolfe. Silby called Robert Pear of the *New York Times*, who seemed interested in writing an article on record group 30. That evening James Demos and I attended a testimonial dinner of a Greek fraternal organization, where we buttonholed Wolfe. He was immediately interested in our story and promised to sponsor a resolution cutting off US aid to the UN if the UNWCC files were not made available to American war crimes investigators.

Before we could proceed Congressman Wolfe quite rightly desired absolute certainty that the files were in fact closed to member governments of the UN. Thus we decided to visit the Israeli mission to the UN to ask them to make an official written request for access to the files. James called the Israeli mission and spoke to Counsellor Yosar Lamdon, who was very happy when he heard that we had uncovered war crimes records at the UN. We made an appointment to visit the Israeli mission to discuss our specific requests. At the time I

1. A copy of the UNWCC list of 40,000 names was found in the US National Archives; see *New York Times*, 14 May 1986. My own investigation reveals that hundreds of copies of the UNWCC list of names were printed in 1949 and distributed to the seventeen member governments of the War Crimes Commission.

naïvely believed that the government of the state of Israel would be anxious to pursue suspected war criminals.

On Friday 7 March 1980 we met Counsellor Lamdon and Ambassador Shabtai Rosenne, who was the chief of the legal section of the Foreign Office and its leading expert on war criminals. Lamdon was a young fellow with an Oxford accent and a self-assured manner. Ambassador Rosenne appeared to be in his seventies and had a long record of service dating back before the birth of the Jewish state in 1948. He was in New York for the Law of the Seas Conference but was taking time to see us. (As with all my meetings, I made handwritten notes afterwards.)

Right from the start, Rosenne was hostile to us. At first he insisted that all war crimes files at the UN were open. In order to impress us he said he had the assurance of YIVO (the Jewish agency) and 'a world-famous expert on this subject' as well as the Israeli Foreign Office. But his bluff did not work, since it appeared strange to me that an Israeli diplomat sitting in the Israeli mission to the UN should have to contact so many outsiders to see if files at the UN were accessible.

Ambassador Rosenne admitted that in 1960 he had been involved in the effort to get UNWCC material for the Eichmann trial. He acknowledged that there had been a 'gentleman's agreement' (his exact words) between Israel and the UN to keep the existence of the UNWCC records secret after the Israelis had secured the file on Eichmann. Rosenne insisted that in 1960 the UNWCC files had been closed but that they were now open. Rosenne refused to state when and by whom they had been opened.

In the middle of our conversation Rosenne was called out of the room for an important phone call. He returned to the conference and triumphantly proclaimed that he now had 'absolute confirmation from the very highest level of the Foreign Ministry in Jerusalem that all war crimes files at the

UN are open'. He implied that Foreign Minister Moshe Dayan, Secretary General Kurt Waldheim and Mr Suy, the assistant secretary general for legal affairs, had all verified that all war crimes files at the UN were open. I was not intimidated by this, however, and stuck to my story.

Although Ambassador Rosenne was my senior in age and status I cut him off: 'Mr Ambassador, I do not wish to seem impertinent,' I said, 'but I am in possession of evidence which clearly shows that there are files that are closed and perhaps it is time to discuss this.' A look of defeat came over the faces of Ambassador Rosenne and his young colleague. From this point the Israeli diplomats made only pro forma attempts to assert that all files were open.

During our interview I kept asking Ambassador Rosenne why he was trying to discourage our efforts. I asked him to take us into his confidence, since we were working with Congressman Wolfe, a friend of Israel. Neither he nor Lamdon would give a straight answer but it was clear that they were covering something up. But what?

When it became obvious that they could not discourage us, Lamdon asked if we had a specific request to make of his mission. I told them that the Yugoslavs were awaiting permission from Belgrade to make a written request to see UNWCC files at the UN. We asked that the Israelis immediately make such a written request so that, if the files really were closed, Congressman Wolfe would secure the assurance he required. But Rosenne and Lamdon refused to do anything without permission from Jerusalem. They said they would ask permission from their government but that it would take time. They could make no official request without permission from their Foreign Office.

I explained that our goal was a General Assembly resolution requiring that record group 30 files be opened upon written request being made by member governments. Despite their earlier claim that the files were already open, both diplomats stated that such a General Assembly resolution would be opposed by the USA, the Soviet bloc and most of Western Europe as well as Israel's enemies in the Third World. (They neglected to mention the Latin American countries which were protecting Nazi war criminals.) In short, any effort to open the files would not be supported by a single member state of the UN.

According to Ambassador Rosenne, most European countries – both East and West – feared to disclose war criminals who had been working for their governments. The Israeli diplomat pointed out quite correctly that even with prodding from Congress, the State Department would never make a serious effort to open up the UN war crimes files.

Despite his insistence that the files were open, everything Ambassador Rosenne said tended to refute his assertion. He spoke poorly of Secretary General Kurt Waldheim who, he said, 'personally favoured keeping all lists of Nazi war criminals secret'. Rosenne listened keenly for my reply to this but the remark went over my head.

When I mentioned Ivan Kerno's 1949 memorandum which recommended keeping parts of the UNWCC files secret, Rosenne answered that he was not surprised, since Ivan Kerno was 'one of the few genuine Fascists ever to serve at the highest echelons of the UN'. (His reference to fascists at 'the highest levels of the UN' was also lost on me.)

During our conversation I showed Ambassador Rosenne a copy of the index to record group 30 which I had obtained from the archivist Erlandson. Rosenne displayed detailed knowledge of the UNWCC files. He boasted that in the 1940s he had helped prepare the Polish UNWCC files on Nazi atrocities against Jews.

Ambassador Rosenne revealed that during the Eichmann affair he had been involved in the effort to obtain documents.

But he noted that the Americans had refused to give Israel access to certain Nazi party membership files. (He may have been hinting that the Americans were holding Nazi organization records on Waldheim but I am not certain of the purpose of this remark. There is no doubt, however, that there was a double meaning in many of the things he said. Rosenne obviously suspected that I knew about Waldheim.)

We left the Israeli mission after Rosenne and Lamdon had promised to look into the status of record group 30. I had little faith in this promise.

That evening I returned home much disturbed. What could be in those files that was such a terrible secret? That evening a call from the Yugoslav UN mission frightened me greatly. A Yugoslav diplomat told me that 'some of the UNWCC files had been shipped to Washington ten years ago'. This would have been around 1971. In 1980 I made no connection with the fact that at that time Kurt Waldheim was being considered for the position of Secretary General. In any case the message was a clever one. If I had known about Waldheim, it would have told me not to bother Yugoslavia about the matter but to go after my own government, which had obtained copies of Waldheim's file. However, if, as was the case, I knew nothing about Waldheim, the message did not reveal the secret.

On 10 March I called the UN legal office. I inquired about the status of the record group 30 files. I was told that the case records against the 40,000 suspects were closed. This would apply to member states as well as private individuals who sought access to the files. I called Rosenne and asked him to call the legal office. He was not at a loss for words. He informed me that over the weekend (when all UN offices were closed) he had made further inquiries and found that the UNWCC files were still classified. His new line was that these files were not important. The testimony of the witnesses was based on hearsay information and the documents were inaccurate. He added that all the good cases had been brought to trial and that the 40,000 had not been prosecuted because the cases against them were not strong. (Adolf Eichmann had been among the 40,000.)

Several days later the *New York Times* called Congressman Wolfe to say that the UN officially stated that the record group 30 files were closed and could be opened only by a General Assembly resolution. Wolfe stated that he would introduce legislation in Congress asking the US ambassador to the UN to look into the matter.

During this time I spoke with Erlandson, who said that representatives of the Justice Department had come to the UN archives indicating that the OSI was seriously interested in record group 30 files. Erlandson told them that they had to make an official application through the US mission to the UN. They said that they would do so. Of course this struck me as odd. The files had been there for thirty years and it was only after I had visited various UN missions that the Justice Department decided it was seriously interested in the UNWCC files. Of course it could have been a coincidence, but it appeared to me that word of my activity had reached the Justice Department and it did not wish to seem inactive in the event of some publicity on this matter.

On the morning of 28 March 1980 I was awakened by the *New York Times* and informed that the article had been published. I was disappointed by the headline, 'US seeks access to UN archives on war criminals in inquiry on Nazis', for it gave the impression that the Justice Department had been vigorously trying to obtain documents which in reality they had deliberately ignored for decades.

Even more shocking was Nazi-hunter Simon Wiesenthal's statement in the story that he 'did not know such records were being kept at the United Nations'. The article stated that there were forty-two linear feet of files on 40,000 suspected criminals. Could it be that Wiesenthal did not know that such a huge collection existed at the UN? (In the months after the article was published, the archivist Erlandson told me that neither Wiesenthal nor anyone from his organization had visited the archives to ask about the files or to examine the open portions of the UNWCC records which the famous Nazi hunter claimed to have overlooked.)[1]

On the afternoon of 28 March James Demos and I held a press conference near the UN which was attended by about forty reporters. I announced that I was looking for additional war crimes records that had disappeared after the Second World War. These were the CROWCASS (Central Registry of War Criminals and Security Suspects) lists. I had come across references to the CROWCASS lists in the open portions of the UNWCC files. I was determined to find the CROWCASS records as well as the list of 40,000 names in the UNWCC files.

At the press conference I was afraid that someone would ask me about Wiesenthal's statement that he didn't know about the UNWCC files. How could anyone believe such an apparent lie? I also feared that they would ask me why neither the USA nor Israel had done anything about the files for so many decades. But the reporters did not put me on the spot with any penetrating questions. Nor did they notice the fact that Erlandson had been ordered out of town by his UN superiors for a 'previously scheduled' vacation. Several

1. In his 1967 book *Murderers Among Us* (p. 188) Wiesenthal wrote: 'Of the 5,000 names on the list of war criminals active in Yugoslavia where 2 million people were killed, 2,499 were Austrians.' Apparently Wiesenthal had a copy of the list which contained the names of the 2,499 Austrians accused of crimes in Yugoslavia. He must surely have noticed the name of Waldheim, who in the 1960s was Austrian ambassador to the UN. As we shall see, Waldheim's hidden war-time service in Yugoslavia was common knowledge among informed people in Vienna.

journalists who attended the press conference, including the Reuters and BBC correspondent, filed reports on the press conference.

That morning there had been a press conference at the US mission to the UN. They held to the story that the US mission had requested the files but that they had been turned down by the Secretariat. But the next day I learned that there had been a private briefing at the UN for diplomats from various interested governments. A UN spokesman told the diplomats that the Justice Department had not asked for the files until after the *New York Times* article had appeared. The story the Justice Department had given to the press – that it had already asked for the files – was a fabrication. When the US mission had belatedly made its request, the UN had replied that the subject was open for consideration.

On 31 March 1980, a few days after the *New York Times* article appeared, I was called by Ambassador Rosenne. He was very angry about the stories that were appearing in the press. He read me a telegram from the Israeli Foreign Ministry in Jerusalem. According to Ambassador Rosenne, it stated: 'The Israeli government has experienced no difficulty in obtaining material from the War Crimes Commission records.' He was very evasive as to the meaning of the message. When I asked him if it meant that Israel had secretly obtained information from the UNWCC archives, he answered yes.

Ambassador Rosenne called my actions 'suspicious' but he refused to explain what he suspected me of. He also accused me of inspiring the *New York Times* story. I indicated that since I was mentioned in almost every paragraph my connection with the *New York Times* story was no secret. I stressed that I had acted openly and I had nothing to hide. He never gave me any explanation for his angry tone. He hinted that Simon Wiesenthal's statement that he (Wiesenthal) did not know about the UNWCC files should not be taken literally. Ambassador Rosenne also correctly contradicted the *New York Times* report that the US government had been denied access to the UNWCC records.

Ambassador Rosenne's most startling statement was that all the responsible Nazi war criminals had been prosecuted immediately after the Second World War. He said that the Israelis considered the question of war criminals to be closed and were not interested in pursuing any more Nazi murderers. I shall never forget the uneasiness in his voice when he made this statement.

The attitude of Ambassador Rosenne disturbed me, but the Israeli government was not alone in its effort to cover up the UN war crimes files. The US mission to the UN had a similar attitude. Several days after Rosenne's call I visited the UN to meet Keith Hindell of the BBC who took an interest in my story. He agreed with me that there must be something very important in the UNWCC files and he was trying to interest his network in making a film documentary on the subject. After my meeting with the foreign correspondent I called Robert Rosenstock, the legal officer of the US mission to the UN.

Publicly, Rosenstock was claiming to be making an effort to gain access to the files for use by the Justice Department. I doubted the sincerity of his efforts, but I thought it my duty to offer assistance. When I contacted Rosenstock by phone I identified myself and said that I had considerable knowledge about the UNWCC records. 'Oh, we have no doubt that you are knowledgeable,' he replied in a sarcastic tone. I offered to make an appointment and to turn over to him copies of UN documents which would strengthen any case made by the USA to gain access to the files. Rosenstock turned my offer down. He even refused to accept copies of UN documents I offered to mail to him and then he hung up. This was my only contact with the US mission to the UN, but it told me what I wanted to know.

During this period the Law of the Seas Conference brought to New York many legal experts from around the world besides Ambassador Rosenne. Among them was Constantine Stravopolous (who has since died). Stravopolous had served on the original UNWCC and later became an Assistant Secretary General of the UN for legal affairs. Through James Demos's Greek contacts we obtained an interview with Stravopolous, who had indicated that he wanted to speak to us. He proved to be just as anxious as the Israelis to keep a lid on the record group 30.

For over an hour he abused and intimidated me. He called me a 'red agitator' (which I am not). He said I should write a book on Soviet atrocities in Afghanistan or crimes of Greek Communists during the civil war. His Cold War attitude surprised and disappointed me since I had been told that he had been a man of great influence at the UN. When Stravopolous saw that I could not be intimidated (at one point I laughed at his threats and insults) he tried to appeal to James Demos on the basis of Greek solidarity. But James also stood his ground.

It was clear that Stravopolous knew the secret of the UNWCC files. His performance reinforced my conviction that there was something very important in these files but I still could not figure out what everyone was trying to cover up.

By this point I realized that my plan to open the files through political pressure was hopeless. I turned next to the news media but once again I found little support. The one exception was Keith Hindell of the BBC who liked my idea for a TV documentary on the war crimes files. I made out a proposal and it was approved by several executives in his network. However, the project was shot down by the BBC's leading 'war crimes expert'. He had assured the directors that there couldn't be anything of importance in the UNWCC files. I continued, however, to keep Keith Hindell informed of my efforts to gain access to the UNWCC files.[1]

I tried a different approach. On 7 May, Gideon Hausner, the prosecutor in the Eichmann trial of 1962, came to speak at the City University of New York. As a member of the Israel Knesset and as director of Yad Vashem, Hausner was the leading Israeli authority on war criminals. I believed that he could help explain the attitude of the Israeli UN mission towards record group 30. After his lecture I approached Hausner, who said he had read the story in the *New York Times* and wanted to speak to me. He indicated he was going back to Israel the next evening but he took my number and said he would call me at home.

The next morning I received a call from Hausner. He confirmed that when he prosecuted Eichmann in 1962 he had obtained files on the Nazi murderer from the UN. He indicated surprise when I told him about Ambassador Rosenne's attitude. He asked me to write a report since he could 'only act on written information'.

I sent a report to Hausner outlining my contact with the Israeli UN mission. Soon after, I received a reply from him. He promised to 'pursue the matter further' and thus get an explanation from the Israeli Foreign Ministry as to their attitude toward the UN war crimes files. He denied, without an investigation, Rosenne's statement that Israel was not interested in apprehending Nazi war criminals, since 'even very recently' an extradition request had been made 'with regard to such a person in Brazil' (Mengele?). Hausner ended by once again promising to 'clarify all the points in my letter'.[2]

There is no doubt that, soon after, Hausner did make

1. In May 1986 Keith Hindell wrote an article in the London *Times* based on my 1980 experiences. See page 149.
2. Copy of letter in my possession.

inquiries at the Foreign Ministry about why the Israeli mission to the UN was covering up the UNWCC files. However, after making these inquiries, Hausner refused to give me an explanation or even answer any more of my letters. It seems that Hausner learned the truth about what was in the UN war crimes files. Having done so, he could not discuss the matter with me or anyone else.[1]

Hausner's failure to answer my letters increased my suspicions about the files.

On 27 May, I spoke to P. Kirsch of the Canadian UN mission. He indicated that the USA had received some files from the UNWCC records (this was a story then circulating at the UN) and that the Canadians were considering asking for access since they had several hundred war criminals in their country. He told me that when he spoke to the UN legal office they informed him that the files had been kept secret at the request of the member states of the UNWCC and that all the prima facie cases had been sent back to the countries involved, thus leaving in the UN archives only records of the unsubstantiated cases. I was angry but not surprised that the UN was still handing out such nonsense.

The next day I went to Washington for a meeting with Jim Switzer, an aide to Congresswoman Elizabeth Holtzman on her judiciary sub-committee. He said that the story that the UN had given the Justice Department access to the record group 30 files was exaggerated. I told him that I wished to call

1. In May 1986 Hausner was contacted by an Israeli news-magazine. Both he and Gabriel Bach, his chief aide during the Eichmann trial, denied that they had received documents on the Nazi butcher from record group 30, despite the recent admission of the Israeli UN mission indicating that their country indeed received files on Eichmann from the Secretariat. The refusal of Hausner even to admit what is public information led a well-known Israeli journalist to suspect a cover-up: Tom Segev, 'Did we blackmail Waldheim?', *Koteret Rashit*, 21 May 1986. See also Keith Hindell, 'Waldheim: a question mark over Israel', *The Times* (London), 13 May 1986.

another news conference, but he urged me not to since this might 'jeopardize further US efforts to gain additional access to the files'. I was convinced that the publicity I had generated had, if anything, helped stimulate what action had already been taken with regard to the files, but I agreed not to hold another press conference.

The congressional aide seemed to be well informed about the situation at the UN. In my notes I wrote: 'Jim Switzer said that the US mission to the UN had pretended [at first] that there was no problem and that all the files were open. This was the same line that the Israeli mission to the UN had taken. It seems clear that they were working together.' Switzer helped make an appointment for me to see Alan Ryan, head of the OSI in the Justice Department. Before leaving Washington, I spoke to another congressional aide who was knowledgeable about war crimes investigation. I wrote in my notes: 'He confirmed that S. Wiesenthal lied when he said he knew nothing about the files.'

On 5 June I returned to Washington. I wished to begin my search for the CROWCASS lists. Since I had been lucky enough to find the UNWCC files, I felt that with some effort I could locate this other important document collection. I first went to see Alan Ryan. He asked me what I was after. I told him honestly that I wanted to find the CROWCASS list so that I could check the names against US immigration records, since I had a very good contact at the Immigration and Naturalization Service. Ryan said that he had the CROWCASS list and was already checking it against immigration records to see if any war criminals had entered the USA illegally by concealing their past. Ryan also indicated that he had the UNWCC list, which in 1986 was revealed to also contain Kurt Waldheim's name.[1]

1. In 1986 the OSI consistently denied having the UNWCC list of 40,000

The chief of OSI indicated, however, that whereas he had the CROWCASS list of detained and wanted war criminals, he lacked the supporting CROWCASS files which gave a physical description of each suspect. (Since, like the UNWCC files, the CROWCASS list contained the name Kurt Waldheim, Ryan may have desired the actual CROW-CASS files to see if the physical description of the Kurt Waldheim listed matched the UN Secretary General. The name Waldheim is fairly common.)

After the meeting with Ryan, I thought that OSI would take some action with regard to the UNWCC records. However, I was convinced that the USA, Israel and other nations were trying to protect one or more names on the list. I had no doubt that what was hidden would become public sometime in the future, but I saw no way of finding out who was being protected. I failed to realize that hundreds of copies of the 40,000 names had been printed and that the UNWCC list could be found in the US National Archives and the Public Record Office in London as well as numerous other archives and libraries.

With hundreds of copies of the UNWCC files and perhaps an even greater number of CROWCASS ledgers in circulation, it was very easy for the Israelis to obtain copies of these two important lists, both of which contained the name of the UN Secretary General. It is routine procedure for Mossad (Israeli intelligence) to check the name of any official such as Waldheim who was known to have served in the Wehrmacht.[1]

---

names. But in a book completed in 1985 (Gerald C. Posner and John Ware, *Mengele*, p. 331) the authors indicate that they obtained information on Mengele from the 'United Nations War Crimes List, number 8, maintained by Office of Special Investigations, Washington DC'.

1. For example, in 1965 when Rolf Pauls was appointed the first West German Ambassador to Israel, his Wehrmacht service in Russia was carefully checked by Israeli intelligence. Inge Deutschron, *Berlin and Jerusalem: The Strange Coalition*, p. 337.

The Israeli journalist Tom Segev, who investigated my story, noted that an informant who worked in the Israeli UN mission in 1980 reported that 'there were constant rumours in the delegation about Waldheim's past and about someone in Jerusalem or Tel Aviv who knew him'.[1] Several sources have confirmed to me that the Israeli Foreign Office did know about Waldheim's UNWCC file for many years. Indeed it would have been almost impossible for them to avoid knowing.

It is painful for me to admit that I was constantly stumbling across the secret. While doing research on the operations of the Italian army in Yugoslavia in 1942, I used many German documents, some of which were signed 'Lieutenant Waldheim'. I joked with friends about the name but we agreed 'Waldheim is such a common name!'

At about the time I met Keith Hindell of the BBC for lunch, Keith read a story he was doing on Secretary General Waldheim's background. At this point I was very preoccupied with the secret of record group 30. I remember thinking to myself that Waldheim's biography is all very interesting but let's try to figure out what is being hidden in the UN archives! Somewhat later, on a trip to Washington to discuss the UNWCC with a congressional staffer, he noted that there were rumours about Waldheim's military service but I saw no connection between all this and the UNWCC list of suspected war criminals.

Waldheim's greatest protection lay in the sheer absurdity of the situation. Who would believe that the UN archives contained a *bogus* war crimes file, specifically prepared to blackmail the Secretary General of the UN? I received many hints that Waldheim was impeding war crime investigations, but I thought that the Secretary General was trying to protect

1. Tom Segev, 'Did we blackmail Waldheim?', *Koteret Rashit*, 21 May 1986.

cronies in Austria. In the years between 1980 and 1986, while working on other projects, I made a dozen visits to the section of the National Archives where the UNWCC list was later found. Indeed in 1981 I actually located in a Public Record Office index reference to 'the United Nations War Crimes List', but I thought it referred to routine correspondence about the list since I could not believe that the actual register of 40,000 names could be available on the open shelf!

Given the numbers of copies of the UNWCC and CROW-CASS lists readily available, the US Justice Department, Simon Wiesenthal and Israeli intelligence were not the only ones to possess this important information. As we shall see, the Soviet Union and Yugoslavia also definitely knew about Waldheim's UNWCC file since these two countries worked together in 1947 to fabricate the false war crimes dossier.

It is, of course, difficult for many people to believe that Israel was involved with Waldheim. For decades the Zionists have used Nazi war crimes as a major justification for the Jewish state. But Israel's record of pursuing war criminals has been more apparent than real. According to Tom Segev, 'The prosecution of war criminals was never one of Israel's top priorities. Much was said about it. In reality little was done.' Like the other countries involved Israel has used war crimes information in the Waldheim and many other cases for political purposes.

Of course, since the Austrian presidential election in the spring of 1986 the press has carried a far different Waldheim story including reports that the former Secretary General was 'linked' to Nazi atrocities in Greece and Yugoslavia. In Austria there have been recurring charges that Waldheim's Socialist opponents were responsible for launching the campaign of accusations against him when he ran as the candidate of the Austrian People's Party (OVP). However, Waldheim's chief accusers have been the New York-based World Jewish Congress (WJC) whose president, Edgar Bronfman, has claimed that the former Secretary General had served as 'an important part of Hitler's killing machine'.

Waldheim has been accused on a wide variety of charges. Evidence has been presented that while he attended university he had joined the Nazi student union and the SA (*Sturm Abteilung*) cavalry corps. The most serious charges concern his service with Army Group E in the Balkans from 1942 to 1945. For decades Waldheim hid his service in Greece and Yugoslavia by claiming that he had spent the latter part of the Second World War finishing his degree at the University of Vienna. Waldheim's defence has been to deny all charges including those which were well documented but of no great significance. He has even claimed that he never made an attempt to conceal his past despite the complete omission of his Balkan service from his autobiography and numerous official resumés. Such a strategy has greatly reduced his credibility.

In the spring of 1986, during the Austrian presidential election, there was a constant stream of accusations against Waldheim by the World Jewish Congress. On 2 June 1986, on the eve of the poll, the WJC published a ninety-five-page report which summarized their case against the former UN Secretary General. The report contains a copy of the 1947 UNWCC dossier prepared against Waldheim which claims that he was responsible for 'putting hostages to death' and 'murder'. In addition, the WJC accused Waldheim of being involved in the deportation of Greek Jews and the brutal interrogation of British POWs who were turned over to the SS (*Schutzstaffel*) for execution. There were also allegations that the former Secretary General was involved in the massacre of Yugoslav civilians at Stip-Kočani and Kozara. In September 1986 the WJC added a new charge when they accused

Waldheim of responsibility for German propaganda pamphlets which contained anti-Semitic statements.

In April 1987 the WJC achieved their principal goal when the US Justice Department added Waldheim's name to its 'watch list' of suspected war criminals barred from entry into the USA. The decision was based on a 200-page 'secret report'. Many people have the erroneous impression that the US Justice Department listed Waldheim on the basis of numerous publicly available documents that clearly demonstrate his involvement in a wide variety of atrocities. In reality, however, the situation is quite different. There is, in fact, a consensus among serious military historians and war crimes experts that Lieutenant Kurt Waldheim had no direct involvement with war crimes or crimes against humanity.

It should be realized that over the years very specific definitions have become accepted as the standard for judging whether a soldier has engaged in atrocities and other criminal activity. In 1945 the Allied Occupations Authorities in Germany set up two categories of violations – war crimes and crimes against humanity. A war crime constitutes 'violations of the laws and customs of war' such as the mistreatment of prisoners, killing of hostages and plunder of public property. Crimes against humanity include the extermination of Jews and other ethnic minorities. There is, in fact, no proof that Waldheim is guilty of either war crimes or crimes against humanity. Just because Waldheim was in the Balkans where many atrocities were committed does not prove him guilty. It is easy for us today in America and Britain to condemn those who answered the call for military service in the Third Reich. But how many of us would have had the courage to risk death and dishonour for ourselves and our families by refusing to serve in the German Wehrmacht during the Second World War? In 1971, when Waldheim was elected Secretary General, it was publicly known that he had served on the

Russian front in 1941. Nothing he did in Yugoslavia and Greece in the latter part of the war was any worse than his service in Russia as an ordinary soldier, which was not even mentioned by the USSR or any other country when they elected Kurt Waldheim chief of the world organization.

The real Waldheim story began in 1945 when the young Wehrmacht officer was interrogated by the US Army and recruited for Western intelligence. Shortly afterwards, in occupied Austria, Waldheim was hired for the Vienna Foreign Office by Fritz Molden, the son-in-law of CIA chief, Allen Dulles. Molden assigned the aspiring young diplomat to work as confidential aide to Foreign Minister Karl Gruber, who also had close links with Western intelligence.

In an effort to penetrate the Vienna Foreign Office, in 1947 Yugoslav and Soviet security agents created a bogus war crimes dossier designed to blackmail Waldheim, who had access to most of Gruber's private papers. For decades Waldheim hid his service in the Balkans during the Second World War because he feared revelation of the fraudulent UNWCC file prepared against him by the Yugoslavs. Why did he fear it so much, if it was so obviously fraudulent?

As we shall see, from the example of others in his early years Waldheim had reason to believe that even obviously phoney Yugoslav charges could lead to his dismissal. Later, as Secretary General he certainly realized that his bogus war crimes file could also be used by Zionists and other groups to wage a political campaign against the United Nations and Austria, which is in fact what has happened over the past two years.

Like many other officials in post-war Austria, Waldheim was involved in considerable Cold War intrigue, caught between rival intelligence services which operated freely in that small country occupied by both the Soviet Union and the Western powers. Waldheim also maintained close relations with the Tito government as well as separatist elements in Yugoslavia.

In 1971, during the era of *détente*, Kurt Waldheim with his ties to both superpowers was the ideal candidate for Secretary General of the UN. The false war crimes file in the UN archives made Waldheim controllable, unlike Dag Hammarskjöld and U Thant who had antagonized the superpowers while they were in office. As Secretary General, Waldheim served the interests of the United States and the Soviet Union; indeed, in his memoirs he wrote, 'East–West rivalries while still predominant in global terms have become relatively less prominent in United Nations affairs.' The real struggle in the UN in the 1970s was often between the superpowers against the Third World-controlled General Assembly. In many crisis situations Waldheim served the interests of his American and Soviet patrons.

There is a myth that Waldheim opposed Israel and that he was responsible for the 1975 General Assembly resolution condemning Zionism as a form of racism. In point of fact Waldheim spoke out both privately and publicly against the 1975 resolution and prevented any further General Assembly condemnations of Israel. Waldheim's efforts to placate Israel were not unrelated to its possible possession of documents on the Secretary General's hidden past which, while not criminal, is certainly embarrassing. Waldheim fully realized that the publication of his bogus UN war crimes file by Israel, the United states, Yugoslavia or the Soviet Union would have ensured his resignation as Secretary General.

A study of the Waldheim affair is a unique opportunity to see how the game of nations is played at its most cynical. At the centre of the drama is Kurt Waldheim, a man whose concealed past is the subject of considerable controversy.

CHAPTER I

The Student Years

In his memoirs Kurt Waldheim portrays himself as a dedicated anti-Nazi who never made any compromises with the regime after Hitler annexed Austria in 1938. A close examination of the record reveals that although this is not quite accurate it is nevertheless totally inaccurate to describe Kurt Waldheim as a Nazi. Waldheim never joined the Nazi party and as a result was always under suspicion.

The future Secretary General and President of the Austrian Republic was born in 1918, the year in which the Habsburg Austro-Hungarian monarchy collapsed. The young Kurt Waldheim grew up in a small independent Austria bordering a Germany which also lay restive after defeat in the First World War. Many in Germany and Austria desired revenge and the union of all German-speaking people. In 1933, with the advent of the Hitler regime in Berlin, there was intensive agitation by National Socialists on both sides of the border who favoured the *Anschluss* (union) of Austria with the German Reich.

Waldheim has long rightly pointed out that he came from a family which was anti-Nazi. His father, a district school inspector, was dismissed from his post because of his outspoken support of Chancellor Kurt von Schuschnigg who opposed the union of his country with Nazi Germany. But in March 1938 the *Anschluss* of Germany and Austria was achieved when Nazi troops occupied the small republic. In 1938 the twenty-year-old Kurt Waldheim was studying at the Vienna Consular Academy, a prestigious institution which prepared students for careers in diplomacy and law.

On 1 April 1938, a few weeks after the *Anschluss*, Kurt

Waldheim joined the Nazi student union. This was practically compulsory for any university student under the Nazi regime and does not necessarily indicate any ideological commitment. The Nazi student union had control over every aspect of university life in the Third Reich; indeed many joined simply to get a room in a dormitory.[1]

But membership of the student union was not sufficient to maintain one's status in an institution of higher education under the Third Reich, since 'the university student was expected to hold his own as a member of the Hitler Youth, the SA or SS'.[2] Waldheim had long been interested in riding; indeed in 1936 he had done his compulsory military service in the cavalry corps of the Austrian Republic. Thus, on 18 November 1938 he joined the SA cavalry corps.

The SA of 1938 scarcely resembled the storm troopers who helped Hitler to power. In 1934 the SA had been emasculated, its influence largely passing to the SS. According to the Nuremberg Judgment, after 1934 the SA was 'a group of unimportant hangers-on'.[3] The Nuremberg Tribunal did not list the SA as a Nazi criminal organization. Membership in the SA riding corps did not amount to much. Hubert Freisleben, a former Nazi student leader in Vienna, has noted: 'Anyone belonging to such an SA group was not considered very active. They joined just to show they were joining something. If someone could ride that's where he

1. H. W. Koch, *The Hitler Youth*, p. 177; *Profil*, 3 March 1986; Richard Grunberger, *The 12-Year Reich*, p. 353.
2. David Schoenbaum, *Hitler's Social Revolution*, p. 261. Koch, ibid, p. 177: 'The National Socialist German Student League now replaced corporations and membership became compulsory. At universities complaints increased from staff and students alike regarding the excessive extra-mural activities forced on the students.' Grunberger, ibid. p. 350: 'Only one student out of every four attending university during the Third Reich managed to shirk the many additional duties incumbent upon members of the National Socialist Students' Association.'
3. *Judgment of the International Military Tribunal for the Trial of Nazi Criminals*, p. 80.

went. They were not considered committed.'[1]

It is difficult for many people in America or Britain to understand the great pressure exerted on citizens of a totalitarian regime that controls almost all institutions and organizations. The fact that a person living in Nazi Germany or Soviet Russia joins one or more party-sponsored groups does not necessarily indicate any ideological preference. For example, many anti-Soviet dissidents who have fled from the USSR in recent years joined various party-sponsored organizations in their native land, but this certainly doesn't mean they were Communists. In a totalitarian country it is almost impossible to function as a student or professional without some token involvement with the regime. The key point, however, is that Waldheim never joined or applied for membership to the Nazi party. In the Third Reich eight million people became card-carrying Nazis but Kurt Waldheim was never one of them.[2]

Over the past two years many former classmates and neighbours have testified to the anti-Nazi attitude of Kurt Waldheim and his family. A few of these have been reported in the British news media but not in the American. Perhaps the most impressive has been the testimony of George Lord Weidenfeld of Chelsea, an Austrian Jew who emigrated to Britain where he became prominent in publishing. He asserts that in the 1930s Waldheim was an 'active liberal Catholic and convinced anti-Nazi who came from a conservative Catholic milieu'. He recalls that as a student, Kurt 'voiced definitely anti-racist views and had many Jewish friends'. Weidenfeld believes that Waldheim's behaviour in the 1930s was 'above reproach'.

Weidenfeld knew Waldheim personally and notes that he 'behaved in a friendly manner and was helpful towards me

1. *Profil*, 3 March 1986.
2. Kurt Waldheim's wife joined the party but there is no evidence that she had any influence on her husband.

until my emigration after the *Anschluss*'. He adds 'this was in clear contrast to many opportunists, sycophants and those who hurried to join the side of the Nazis and who turned out to be unfriendly and arrogant towards me'.[1]

Indeed, the former Secretary General's record under the Third Reich does not compare unfavourably to that of most of his contemporaries who made much more open demonstrations of support for the regime. It is Waldheim's concealment of his record, his absurd denials after the facts were revealed, as well as the distortions which have appeared in the British and American press that make his student affiliations seem far more serious than they were.

Much of the information on Waldheim's student affiliations was first uncovered in a series of balanced and well-researched articles in the Austrian magazine *Profil*.[2] The chief investigator Peter Michael Lingens displayed remarkable objectivity despite the fact that his father was sent to a Nazi punishment battalion and his mother was an inmate at Auschwitz. Missing from Lingens's work is the sensational attitude which is so common among British and American reporters or the 'Waldheim right or wrong' attitude of many Austrian journalists.

Lingens points out that honour students could receive a government grant if their political attitude was acceptable to the Nazi regime. Despite his exceptional grades, Waldheim was refused a student grant – almost certainly because of his family's anti-Nazi reputation. Indeed a 1940 Nazi Gauleiter report expressed suspicion of Waldheim's father and

---

1. WB, p. 101.
2. A World Jewish Congress book cites *Profil* for its 'freedom of expression and the independence of its editorial line'. But while praising *Profil* for its many important revelations about Waldheim, the WJC frequently quote the Austrian magazine out of context, ignoring any material that contradicts their sinister image of the former Secretary General. Luc Rosenzweig and Bernard Cohen, *Waldheim*, p. 144; see also WJC report, June 1986, pp. 3–5.

indicated that his son Kurt 'through his braggadocio gave proof of his antipathy towards our movement'.[1] Obviously, young Waldheim was overheard openly criticizing the regime – which was a very unwise practice in the Third Reich.

With the coming of the Second World War, Waldheim served in the German Army. Although for decades he concealed his tour of duty in the Balkans in 1942 to 1945, Waldheim's earlier service, including his participation in the invasion of Russia in 1941, was never hidden. In his memoirs he writes, 'There was no escape from military service' and 'the alternative to being called up was execution'.[2] There are many errors and omissions in Waldheim's memoirs but his claim that he had no way of avoiding military service is correct.

Besides, there was considerable advantage for a man from a family under suspicion to serve in the army. The 1940 Gauleiter report, which was written after Waldheim was drafted into the army, notes that the young man had 'proved himself' through military service which eliminated doubts about his qualification for government service. But despite his higher education, Waldheim would never be trusted with any position of real responsibility in the Wehrmacht.

There is no way to verify Waldheim's claim that in the army 'anti-Nazi literature was circulated clandestinely and I read it all'.[3] It is highly probable, however, that while in the army Waldheim's principal concern was survival rather than politics. In Russia in 1941 Waldheim served in a cavalry squadron of a reconnaissance battalion of the 45th Infantry Division. This was a particularly dangerous assignment since his principal mission was to ride ahead and attract enemy fire in order to pinpoint the Russian positions. Waldheim had not

1. Document 1.
2. Kurt Waldheim, *In the Eye of the Storm*, pp. 16, 40.
3. Ibid, p. 17.

volunteered for such hazardous duty but he was placed in the cavalry unit because of his previous service in the cavalry corps of the Austrian Republic.

Decades later when Waldheim became Secretary General, his well-known military service on the Eastern Front would be used against him by critics. Their real grievance, however, was displeasure at the UN's pro-Palestinian positions especially the 1975 anti-Zionist resolution which Waldheim is erroneously accused of supporting. Waldheim writes: 'apparently in connection with my outspoken attitude with regard to the Middle East problem and my strong defence of the legitimate rights of the Palestinians – although at the same time I equally championed the rights of Israel to exist in recognized and secure boundaries – some circles in the UN attacked me vigorously as having been a Nazi since I served in the German Army.'[1]

While Secretary General, Waldheim was also attacked because of suspected student affiliations in the 1930s. Thus on 19 January 1980 Shirley Hazzard published an article in the liberal *New Republic* which criticized Waldheim for 'taking part in the Nazi Youth Movement'. This accusation was repeated on 27 September by Martin Peretz, the editor in chief of the *New Republic*.

Hazzard appears to have lacked any specific information on Waldheim's past.[2] However, Congressman Stephen Solarz of Brooklyn made inquiries in order to verify Hazzard's accusations. In answer to a letter from Solarz, Waldheim replied: 'It would be odd to say the least if the government of the United

1. Ibid, p. 40.
2. In a letter in January 1981, with reference to her accusations against the Secretary General she notes: 'As a student Waldheim would perforce have had to swear allegiance to the Nazi leadership ... My purpose in mentioning this matter was not to single out Waldheim for special disapprobation for his conduct at that time but precisely to show that there was nothing special about him.' Hillel Seidman, *United Nations: Perfidy and Perversion*, pp. 39–40.

States and all the member governments voted twice to elect me as Secretary General of the United Nations if they had been in doubt as to my character and background . . . I wish to say that I was never associated in any way with the Nazi Youth Movement.' Waldheim went on to claim: 'I myself was wounded on the Eastern Front and being incapacitated for further service at the front resumed my law studies at Vienna University where I graduated in 1944.'[1] Waldheim's denials to Solarz would come to haunt him in the years ahead.

During this period the attack on Waldheim was led by the octogenarian right-wing Zionist writer and activist Hillel Seidman. Although lacking any real information, Seidman held a press conference at the UN on 9 October 1980 in which he repeated the accusations in the *New Republic* about the Secretary General's supposed membership of the Hitler Youth. Seidman also agitated over Waldheim's service in Russia, accusing the Secretary General of complicity in the extermination of Jews on the Eastern Front; but here again he had no evidence.

In his book published in 1982, Seidman made clear his real reason for attacking the Secretary General.

It was Waldheim who helped transform the world organization into an arena of intrigue and conspiracy against Western democracies (even if some were not aware of it), particularly against the United States. It was he who remade the UN apparatus into a forum for anti-Semitic propaganda that emanated principally from the USSR and the Arab bloc. He placed the sumptuous halls of the world organization at the disposal of Yasser Arafat's terrorist murderers.[2]

Seidman's attacks on Waldheim as the symbol of the UN's anti-Zionist policy foreshadowed the campaign that would be

1. Even more interesting is the reply Solarz received on 31 December 1980 from Fredrick P. Hitz, the legislative counsel of the CIA, who noted that the agency had 'no intelligence reporting on Waldheim's military service', ibid, p. 149.
2. Ibid, p. 137.

waged after 1986. In 1981 while Waldheim was still Secretary General the Israeli UN mission denied that they were responsible for the accusations being made against him by Zionist circles in New York.[1] It is probably true that the Israeli government avoided making any of its information on Waldheim available to supporters of the Jewish state. However, there were rumours about Waldheim floating around the Israeli UN mission, which may have resulted in a leak.

Rumours were also circulating about Waldheim in Vienna. As early as 1970 a right-wing newspaper questioned Waldheim's background. A spokesman for Waldheim's People's Party denied the accusations. In 1983 rumours spread in Vienna that Waldheim had been on the staff of General Löhr in Yugoslavia, a fact known to informed sources in Austria. In the autumn of 1985 George Karp, a former reporter for *Stern*, raised the issue of Waldheim's membership in the student union. Shortly afterwards *Aula*, a right-wing monthly in Graz, published a caricature of Waldheim as an SA rider.[2]

Rumours were still circulating about Waldheim's past in early 1986. On 21 February 1986 Waldheim agreed to have his record in the war archives opened together with that of his Socialist opponent in the Austrian presidential election. Attached to Waldheim's record was a document which mentioned his membership in the Nazi student union and SA riding corps. Waldheim denied membership in the two organizations but could not explain the document found in the archives. Thus began his tortuous defence of his past, which would reveal the incredible ineptitude of a man who played such a prominent role in the world community.

In an interview Waldheim claimed that he may have been

1. *New York Times* (magazine), 13 September 1981.
2. *Profil*, 3 March 1986.

seen riding with SA members, thus giving people the wrong impression. A Waldheim aide suggested that the records in the archives 'could be forgeries perpetrated by the Socialists'. Incredibly Waldheim denied the validity of the documents from the war archives, which included the 1940 Gauleiter report that portrayed him as an anti-Nazi. Obviously, had the documents in the war archives been forged by Waldheim's enemies, the dossier certainly would not have contained a report so favourable to him.

Waldheim has also claimed that he could have been listed by the Nazi student union by mistake, but the handbook for NSDAP organizations makes it clear that no one could be enrolled unless he applied in person.[1] At one point Waldheim even suggested that he later found out he had been listed in the organizations by accident but that he did not object because he did not wish to endanger his family.[2] With each convoluted explanation Waldheim's credibility decreased and his minor infractions almost half a century earlier seemed more serious.

The *Profil* correspondent Peter Michael Lingens, whose parents were persecuted by the Nazis, believed that Waldheim's membership in the SA brownshirt cavalry corps and Nazi student union amounted to very little. He wrote that the *Profil* investigation 'went after the brown elephant and encountered what amounted by Austrian standards to a mosquito'.[3] He adds 'there should be no problem allowing a man who strayed into the SA at age 20 to assume the Austrian Presidency at 67'. However, Lingens believed that Waldheim's concealment of his past, compounded by his absurd denials, is cause for concern. Even worse, Lingens was very unfavourably impressed by Waldheim's loss of

1. *Profil*, 3 March 1986.
2. *Profil*, 10 March 1986.
3. *Profil*, 3 March 1986.

control when confronted with embarrassing information. He found it hard to believe that 'a man aspiring to the office of president inclines to panic in critical situations'. (Lingens did not realize that Waldheim was panic-stricken because he feared that further investigation would lead to the disclosure of the UNWCC file prepared against him by Yugoslavia for purposes of blackmail.) The Austrian journalist concluded, 'Waldheim is not an evil man' and 'I could shake hands with him'.

However, despite mounting evidence Waldheim continued to deny membership of the innocuous Nazi organizations. Two close acquaintances from 1938 identified Waldheim as the tall man in a class photo of a Nazi student organization meeting.[1] In addition, a diary found in the Vienna State Court refers to a form filled out in Waldheim's name in 1940 indicating membership in the SA and the Nazi student union.[2] Waldheim claimed that, as he was in the army, a member of his family must have completed the form for him, adding the incorrect information about the Nazi organization memberships by mistake. But this is not possible because the forms which were part of Waldheim's application for a position as a court clerk had to be completed in person. Furthermore, his military record indicates that Waldheim was on leave at the time the form was submitted.

While denying actual membership in the Nazi groups, Waldheim further decreased his credibility by implying that he participated without actually joining. On 4 April he told Reuters, 'I had a lot of trouble finishing my studies. I said to myself, I can participate and that can keep me there without being attacked.' With regard to the SA riding corps, on 4 May Waldheim told *Der Spiegel*, 'I wanted to keep up appearances.

1. *Profil*, 24 March 1986.
2. Document 2.

Riding with them did not seem a problem to me. It even seemed useful. It helped me to be considered politically reliable.' Few people in Britain or America believed such explanations just as they would not believe Waldheim's denials of committing atrocities in Greece and Yugoslavia.

Waldheim was able to conceal his service in the Balkans in the latter part of the Second World War by claiming that he spent the years 1942 to 1944 working on his doctorate of law at the University of Vienna. In reality Waldheim completed his dissertation while on leave from his service in Army Group E. In his memoirs he correctly points out that the subject of his thesis was Konstantin Frantz, a nineteenth-century Austrian publicist who favoured a federalist solution to the problem of German unification.[1]

The topic had been chosen for Waldheim by his mentor, a man with connections in the Austrian anti-Nazi resistance movement, Professor Alfred Verdross, who had been forbidden by the regime to teach certain subjects.[2] Together with other select students with anti-Nazi views, Waldheim attended Verdross's private lectures. The eminent professor had chosen Konstantin Frantz as a subject for Waldheim because the nineteenth-century writer espoused the type of federalism and international co-operation that were themes for Waldheim's entire career.

The World Jewish Congress have suggested that Waldheim's dissertation shows that the former Secretary General was a Nazi supporter. Waldheim refers to 'the current great conflict of the Reich with the non-European world'

1. Waldheim, *In the Eye of the Storm*, p. 18.
2. Verdross was a founding member of the anti-Nazi underground resistance organization, Provisorisches Österreichisches Nationalkomitee (POEN). Otto Molden, *Der Ruf des Gewissens – der österreichische Freiheitskampf 1938–1945*, p. 177.

and to the 'magnificent collaboration of all the peoples of Europe under the leadership of the Reich ... against the danger from the East'. These statements, however, do not suggest that Waldheim was a Nazi. It was definitely compulsory for a serving military officer to make a positive reference to the war effort. Indeed, many Germans and Austrians who were not Nazis favoured the struggle in the East, which they saw as a conflict against atheistic Communism. Waldheim obviously regarded the alliance system built by the German Reich in the Second World War as in some sense a realization of the *Volksgemeinschaft* (community of peoples) described by Konstantin Frantz. Clearly Waldheim's praise of Germany's unification of Europe against Soviet Russia suggests that Waldheim was anti-Communist but not necessarily pro-Nazi.

Historian Gordon Craig has pointed out a much more significant fact about Waldheim's dissertation.[1] Konstantin Frantz was a notorious anti-Semite who described the Jews as the most serious threat to the political and moral integrity of the Western world. Waldheim's dissertation was an analysis of Frantz's work *Der Föderalismus*, which has long passages where the author expounds his racist invectives. Waldheim could have gained favour with the regime if he had praised the anti-Semitic portion of Frantz's book but he fails to mention it. Craig believes that Waldheim 'found those parts of Frantz's work both distasteful and irrational whereas on the other hand he was fascinated, as the second part of his dissertation shows, by what Frantz had to say about the possibility of a federal political structure creating not only new forms of law but a new international consciousness.'

A student who conspicuously avoided praising anti-Semitism was practically committing treason in the University of Vienna since Austrian schools of higher education were

1. *New York Review of Books*, 9 October 1986

'the pacemakers of Jew-baiting' in the Third Reich.[1] This was particularly risky for Kurt Waldheim, who was under suspicion because of the outspoken anti-Nazi views of his father.

It is never easy to look into a man's soul but from the evidence available there is no reason to believe that Waldheim ever supported Nazism. Because of his father's anti-Nazi record, the young Waldheim had to be careful not to oppose the regime openly. There was no way for him to avoid some small compromises such as his Nazi student affiliations. His denials after the facts became known were probably motivated by a feeling that the innocuous Nazi organization memberships would appear significant in countries such as the USA and Britain. But Waldheim's strategy has not worked well since his bungling denials have only fuelled suspicion. The former Secretary General's inept defence would be even more apparent in his effort to fend off charges that he committed war crimes during his service in the Balkans.

1. Grunberger, *The 12-Year Reich*, p. 336.

CHAPTER II

The Staff Officer

Much that has appeared in the news media about Kurt Waldheim's military service in the Balkans is misleading. Clearly Waldheim has lied and continues to lie, particularly about his knowledge of the deportation of Jews and other atrocities. But there is no proof that he committed war crimes. The Nuremberg Tribunal stated that 'mere knowledge of the happening of unlawful acts does not meet the requirements of criminal law'. In the trial of Germans accused of atrocities in Yugoslavia, the Tribunal held that a war criminal 'must be one who orders, abets or takes a consenting part in the crime'.[1] Despite a blizzard of accusations and massive research in many countries by several teams of investigators, no documentation has been found against Waldheim which could be used as proof in a court of law. A dispassionate examination of the facts indicates that the former Secretary General was a very junior staff officer with primarily clerical duties who lacked any command powers or real influence.

The Balkan theatre was perhaps the most brutal area of Wehrmacht operations in the Second World War. Unlike North Africa, Italy, Russia or France the principal enemy for the Germans in Yugoslavia was not a regular army but partisans supported by a civilian population. Where they existed at all, battle lines were unclear. In such an environment the Nazis frequently exacted a harsh toll against the civilian population. It should be stressed, however, that Waldheim did not request service in the Balkan theatre. Almost half the

1. *TWC* (Vol. 7: *The Hostage Case*), p. 1286.

Wehrmacht troops in Yugoslavia were Austrian, so that his service there was not at all unusual. Since March 1986 when his hidden past was revealed, Waldheim has admitted his service there but he denies any involvement in war crimes.

Lieutenant Kurt Waldheim's service in Greece and Yugoslavia spanned a three-year period from the spring of 1942 until the end of the war, during which time he was posted to a variety of staff positions. While in the Balkans, Waldheim held the job classification of interpreter (*Dolmetscher*) which was later changed to assistant adjutant (*Ordonnanz Offizier*).[1] As an assistant adjutant, Waldheim served in a number of different positions, including military intelligence officer. This has been the subject of considerable misinformation.

Waldheim's frequent changes of assignment, as well as the numerous leaves he obtained to work on his doctoral dissertation, belie the claims that he was an officer of great significance. Indeed, Waldheim was only a reserve officer who was never a member of the general staff, nor did he hold a regular commission. During his entire period of service in the Balkans he was granted only one promotion – from second lieutenant to first lieutenant, which is not very impressive for a man with his educational background and length of service.

Waldheim's first assignment in the Balkans in March 1942 was with the joint German–Italian Bader Combat Group which operated in the Sarajevo–Dubrovnik area of Yugoslavia. After a severe leg injury in Russia and three months' hospitalization, Waldheim was unfit for service in the field and thus was given a staff job with the Bader Combat Group. His assignment was to act as liaison with the Italians whose

1. *Ordonnanz Offizier* has been given a variety of translations. The World Jewish Congress use 'special missions staff officer', which sounds the most sinister. The recognized German/English military dictionary gives 'assistant adjutant' which is used by David Kahn in his definitive study, *Hitler's Spies – German Military Intelligence in World War II.*

language he spoke fluently. It has been alleged that he acted as interpreter at staff conferences where atrocities were planned.

Newspaper reports suggest that the Justice Department's 'secret report' on Waldheim contains evidence of the deportation of Yugoslav civilians to slave labour in German-occupied Norway, which is supposedly mentioned in the war diary of the *Pusteria* division, while he served as interpreter with that Italian unit. No documents have been produced showing that Waldheim translated at meetings where deportations were planned. Even if this could be demonstrated, such a mechanical function would not be criminal. Of course, these newspaper reports are intended to give a sinister impression of Waldheim's military service in the Balkans.

However, recent testimony gives a different view. A newly published book on Italian military operations during this period notes: 'Many of our officers who belonged to the *Pusteria* Alpine division remember Lt Kurt Waldheim with fondness due to his astonishing anti-Nazi attitude. Capt. Giuseppe Trabattoni, a Milan notary, recalls that the statements and views of the young German liaison officer created a certain embarrassment and a lot of concern among the Italians who were not used to discussing politics in public.'[1] While in the army, Waldheim had not apparently given up his indiscreet and dangerous habit of openly speaking out against the Nazis.

After leaving his assignment as liaison with the *Pusteria* division, Waldheim served during the summer of 1942 as a junior supply officer with the West Bosnian Combat Group stationed at Banja Luka, Yugoslavia. According to the press the US Justice Department's 'secret report' notes that Jews

1. *Le aquile della montagne nere-Storia dell'occupazione della guerra Italiana in Montenegro 1941–43*, p. 318.

were deported to concentration camps from Banja Luka while Waldheim was stationed there. But this is meaningless since there is no evidence that Kurt Waldheim gave the order or was involved.

Perhaps the most persistent accusation against Waldheim is that while he was a supply officer with the West Bosnian Combat Group he participated in the brutal campaign in the Kozara mountains not far from Zagreb, the capital of the Axis puppet state of Croatia. Thousands of Yugoslav civilians were massacred in the Kozara battle and 68,000 other civilians were taken to concentration camps where many of them perished.

Waldheim served in the quartermaster branch at Kozara and it is claimed that he helped process prisoners for deportation to concentration camps. There is also concern about a medal he received after the campaign from the puppet Croatian government, and the fact that Waldheim is listed among thirty-four German soldiers mentioned in a 'commemorative list' for Kozara.[1] Three months after Kozara, Waldheim was promoted to first lieutenant (*Oberleutnant*) and given leave to work on his doctoral dissertation on Konstantin Frantz.

In September 1942, after he returned from his study leave, Waldheim was assigned to the staff of AOK-12 at Arsakli near Salonica, Greece. Waldheim claims that from November 1942 until April 1943 he was in Vienna for another study leave. While Waldheim was in Vienna the staff at Arsakli, which he would eventually rejoin, was designated as the command headquarters of the newly formed Army Group E that would include most of the German troops in the Balkans. It was during the spring of 1943 that the Jewish population of Salonica, only one mile from Arsakli, was rounded up and

1. See Document 3.

The Balkan theatre in the Second World War

shipped to Auschwitz. There has been considerable controversy over whether Waldheim was in Arsakli at the time of the deportations. But whether he was there or not it is impossible to believe his story that he, as a staff officer, did not know about deportations which were common knowledge even to enlisted men throughout the Balkans. Waldheim's persistent denials of knowledge about the extermination of the Jews in the Balkans and other atrocities have created suspicion about his participation.

Lieutenant Kurt Waldheim spent the second quarter of 1943 as a translator working on various liaison tasks with Italian forces in the Balkans. One of these assignments took him to Podgorica, Montenegro, for a meeting on 22 May 1943 between the German Generals Leuters and Phelps and the Italian General Roncaglia.

Many newspapers throughout the world have carried a photograph of translator Lieutenant Kurt Waldheim standing between his superior, Lieutenant Colonel Macholz and Italian General Roncaglia. To the side is SS General Artur Phelps. An effort has been made to use this photograph to associate Waldheim with the SS. There have been erroneous claims that Waldheim's cavalry boots are part of an SS uniform. In fact, Waldheim was never a member of the SS or any other Nazi criminal organization. Waldheim's only possible connection with SS General Phelps would have been to serve as a translator at meetings where the SS general conferred with Italian commanders. But there is no evidence that he even did this.

There is no documentation for the claims that the young lieutenant played a substantive role at meetings where the Axis's allies planned Operation Schwarz (Operation Black) in north-western Montenegro where many atrocities were committed. It is ludicrous to imagine that such a low-ranking reserve officer could have made any substantial contributions at a meeting of generals. Besides, planning for Operation Schwarz had taken place long before 22 May 1943.

It is difficult to understand why so many people could be so convinced that Kurt Waldheim is a war criminal simply because he is in the same photograph as an SS general. This is a classic example of guilt by association which has been exploited by several of the tabloid New York newspapers. Indeed, one newspaper ran a headline, 'Papers show Waldheim was SS butcher' without presenting any evidence that the former Wehrmacht lieutenant was a member of any Nazi criminal organization.[1]

In July 1943, after twenty years of Fascist rule, the Mussolini regime in Italy collapsed, to be replaced by a government headed by Marshal Pietro Badoglio. The Germans rightly suspected that Badoglio planned to defect from the Nazi–Fascist Axis alliance. Accordingly, it was decided to keep a close watch on Italian military formations. A small German staff under General von Gyldenfeldt was assigned to serve as liaison with the Italian 11th Army in Athens. Lieutenant Kurt Waldheim was posted as an assistant adjutant to Lieutenant Colonel Willers of the German liaison staff.

Numerous charges have been made against Waldheim concerning his service in Athens, including one that he was involved in the deportation of Jews from the Greek capital. In due course we shall examine closely the persistent accusations that Waldheim participated in the persecution of Jews. There is no doubt, however, that while in Athens one of Waldheim's duties was to keep the war journal of the liaison staff in which he recorded orders being sent to the German 1st Mountain Division for the execution of captured partisans and the deportation for forced labour of 'suspected partisans and all male civilians'. The June 1986 WJC report (p. 26)

1. *New York Post*, 26 March 1986.

accuses Waldheim of involvement in 'patently criminal orders'.

But the war journal recorded only orders that were sent by higher authorities to field units. Waldheim did not play any role in the formulation of orders recorded in the war journal. Besides, contrary to popular belief, the execution of captured partisans was not a war crime. In the case of Field Marshal List, the Nuremberg Tribunal found that Yugoslav partisans 'were not lawful belligerents entitling them to prisoner of war status upon capture. We are obliged to hold that such guerrillas were *francs-tireurs* who upon capture could be subjected to the death penalty.'[1] It is not even certain that measures taken against suspected partisans were criminal since the Tribunal held that in Yugoslavia the Germans were 'entitled to take precautions against those suspected of participation in the resistance movement' and that 'as a last resort hostages and reprisal prisoners may be shot.'[2] In the most extreme circumstances, the use of suspected partisans as forced labour by way of reprisal was not necessarily criminal. At any rate, clearly Waldheim did not take part in the activities he recorded in the war journal. It is thus misleading to imply he was responsible for the criminal orders.

Waldheim is accused of being involved, while he was in Athens, in the transportation of Italian POWs to labour camps after Marshal Badoglio signed an armistice with the Allies. As in so many other cases, as we shall see, Waldheim's culpability in war crimes against Italian POWs is more apparent than real.

After liquidation of the Italian 11th Army, Waldheim returned to Army Group E headquarters in Arsakli where he

---

1. *TWC* (Vol. 7, *The Hostage Case*), p. 1273.
2. Ibid, p. 1273.

was assigned to the Ic/AO (Military intelligence/counter-intelligence) group of the army group staff. The young lieutenant was posted as an '03' (intelligence staff officer) serving under the chief of the Ic/AO, Lieutenant Colonel Herbert Warnstorff. There has been considerable misinformation in the news media about Waldheim's service with the Ic/AO group at Arsakli. Most of the press reports on Waldheim fail to point out that the Ic/AO was divided into two autonomous sections, an Ic intelligence (*Feindnachrichten*) and an AO-counter intelligence (*Abwehr*) unit which dealt with propaganda, reprisals, deportations of Jews, relations with the SS and all other 'political matters'. As the 1 December 1943 organization chart of the Ic/AO group indicates, Kurt Waldheim was responsible for the evaluation of enemy intelligence and other duties that we shall consider.[1]

As commander of the entire Ic/AO group Lieutenant Colonel Warnstorff supervised both the AO and Ic units. The organization chart indicates that he shared a wide range of activities with his deputy, Major Hammer. There appears to have been a secret agreement between Lieutenant Colonel Warnstorff and Major Hammer whereby the commander took responsibility for 'political matters, co-operation with the SS, security police and field gendarmerie' and his deputy handled other duties.[2] Despite this arrangement, there are documents which indicate that Hammer was involved with the SS and the deportation of Jews. There are, however, no documents showing that Lieutenant Kurt Waldheim of the Ic staff took part in propaganda, reprisals, police or other Abwehr 'political matters'.

However, there can be little doubt that Waldheim and his

1. Document 4.
2. According to the Salzburg historian Gerhard Botz, the secret agreement between Warnstorff and Hammer was made on 1 December 1943, the same day the Ic/AO organization chart was drawn up: *Profil*, 25 May 1986.

colleagues in the Ic unit had some idea of what the Abwehr was up to. The 03 had to know that the Abwehr was involved in the deportation of Jews, propaganda and other non-military duties. Waldheim has pointed out that the Abwehr worked in secrecy and isolation. This is probably quite true but it would have helped his credibility to have admitted that, while he did not participate, he knew the Abwehr unit was involved in some rather criminal dealings.

Amidst all the concern about whether Waldheim committed war crimes, the young lieutenant's involvement in intelligence matters has been overlooked. In particular, it is necessary to consider Waldheim's knowledge of the negotiations in March 1943 between the German High Command and representatives of Tito's partisans. An important part of Waldheim's duties was to evaluate the intentions of the partisans so that he surely had access to the German reports of the meetings, which belie the Yugoslav dictator's claim that during the war he never offered to collaborate with the Axis occupiers.

In these years there was constant manoeuvring in Yugoslavia between the Germans, the Italians, the pro-Axis Croatian puppet government, the right-wing Chetnik resistance forces and the Communist partisans. Official Yugoslav Communist party mythology maintains that unlike the Chetnik leader Draža Mihailovic, Tito never entered into any treasonable negotiations with the Fascist enemy. However, on 11 March 1943 a partisan delegation, including (the future Yugoslav dissident) Milovan Djilas made a far-reaching offer to a German delegation headed by Lieutenant General Benignus Dippold. The partisans suggested that 'it would be in the interest of both sides if hostilities ceased. In connection with the German headquarters, this delegation should determine proposals concerning a possible [non-combat] zone and lay down aims for economic and other interests.[1] Tito's representatives even offered that the partisans 'would also take up combat against the English if the latter would land' in the Balkans. On Hitler's order the Germans broke off the negotiations with Tito.

The record of the negotiations between Tito and the Germans would have been political dynamite in post-war Yugoslavia where the dictator conducted a much-publicized trial of the Chetnik leader Mihailovic on charges of treason and collaboration. Waldheim's access to the documents which proved that Tito himself attempted to collaborate with the Germans is an important but much neglected piece in the Waldheim puzzle.

Equally significant is the military intelligence which Waldheim acquired while working as an 03 in the Ic unit. He became an expert on Yugoslavia – knowledge which would be highly prized in the tense post-war world. It is unfortunate that the significance of this aspect of the former Secretary General's background has been lost in the many war crimes charges against him.

The first accusations against Waldheim were made in 1947 in a file submitted to the United Nations War Crimes Commission (UNWCC) by Yugoslavia. Waldheim was charged with 'putting hostages to death' and 'murder'.[2] The sole evidence is the testimony of Johann Mayer and Klaus Melinschoff, former members of the staff of Army Group E. The Yugoslavs produced no documents to support the statements of the German POWs.

The value of this testimony must be evaluated in the light of the treatment of German POWs by the partisans. Though Yugoslavs are reluctant to admit it, captured Wehrmacht

---

1. NA: T-119/16/75-81.
2. For a copy of Waldheim's UNWCC dossier, see Document 5.

personnel were subject to extreme brutality designed to pay back the Germans since the Nazis classified partisan prisoners as 'bandits' not covered by the Geneva Convention. No quarter was given by either side in the savage partisan war. According to a US army intelligence report, when Wehrmacht soldiers were taken by Tito's forces, 'the sick and the wounded would be slain in their beds' while the partisans 'would mutilate both the living and the dead in exacting personal vengeance'.[1]

Johann Mayer and Klaus Melinschoff, the prisoners who signed statements against Waldheim, were among the tens of thousands of Wehrmacht personnel captured by the Yugoslavs at the end of the Second World War when Army Group E surrendered. The fate of these German POWs in 1945 is described in a recent book by James Lucas, a staff member of the Imperial War Museum in London.[2] According to Lucas, when the men in Army Group E realized that they would be handed over to the Communist partisan army, hundreds of German soldiers committed suicide. The Yugoslavs were determined to make the Germans pay with interest for every drop of blood they had spilt during the brutal partisan war. Tito ordered a 2,000-kilometre 'march of expiation' in which the defenceless German prisoners were shot, stabbed and burned alive in some of the worst atrocities of the war. In June 1945 a British witness to the trek of death reported 'one of the most beastly scenes I have ever seen. Many were barefoot, starving, haggard, with a large percentage suffering from dysentery and even typhus.

---

1. *German Anti-Guerrilla Operations in the Balkans 1941–1944*, Department of Army, German report series pamphlet 20-243, p. 34. The Nuremberg Military Tribunal noted 'That German prisoners captured by the resistance forces [in Yugoslavia] were tortured, mutilated and killed is shown by the evidence.': TWC (Vol. 7, *The Hostage Case*), p. 1273.
2. James Lucas, *The Last Days of the Reich*, pp. 119–142.

To the delight of the populace, the laggards were kicked by Partisans.'[12]

Lucas estimates that in the first few months 60 per cent of the German prisoners were massacred. The survivors of the trek of death were treated to further tortures which would permanently impair their health. No distinction was made between the guilty and the innocent since the Yugoslavs considered all Germans war criminals – including female nurses.

Indeed, most of the Wehrmacht POWs who survived the death march were placed in 're-education camps' where they suffered brutal interrogation. In 1948 Johann Mayer returned to Austria and told his wife that while in Yugoslav captivity he had observed the 'Golden Rule'. This was the practice of all members of Army Group E never to incriminate any fellow POW but to blame all atrocities on officers such as Waldheim who were not in captivity and therefore were assumed to be dead or safely at home.

Clearly in such conditions the testimony of Wehrmacht POWs held by the Yugoslavs cannot be taken seriously. There are in fact many other reasons which make it clear that Waldheim's UNWCC file is worthless. This dossier is based on a resolution (*Odluka*) submitted to the UNWCC's Committee I on Facts and Evidence by the Yugoslav National War Crimes Commission.[3] The Yugoslav *Odluka* against Waldheim was received by the UNWCC on 19 February 1948 and given to Committee I, which evaluated the evidence and determined whether an accused should be placed on its

1. PRO: FO 371–48909. Another report noted: 'It is not only the Germans who are ill-treated. Very similar handling is given to their own underlings ... Sheer insensibility seems to be inherent in the character of these people.': FO 371–48906.
2. *Profil*, 7 April 1986.
3. See Document 6.

roster of suspected war criminals. No documents were submitted by the Yugoslavs indicating that Waldheim had committed war crimes.

The only evidence in the *Odluka* comprises the statements of Johann Mayer and Klaus Melinschoff. Committee I made every effort to accommodate the request of a member state of the UNWCC that an accused person be placed on the list of suspects. Indeed the statements of Mayer and Melinschoff against Waldheim were changed either by the Yugoslavs or UNWCC staff members to make them sound much more incriminating. In his original declaration quoted in the Yugoslav *Odluka* Johann Mayer stated:

I am aware that on one occasion in Sarajevo certain civilians were killed; though it was a question of German soldiers who had deserted and who had created an anti-fascist organization. Orders for shooting them were issued by Section Ic, according to information from the Gestapo . . . This order was issued by the Chief of the General Staff and the Commander of the Army Group. This was in November/December 1944.

Note that in this statement Mayer does not even mention Waldheim's name. But in Waldheim's UNWCC dossier this has been changed to:

I remember certain persons having been murdered at Sarajevo in November 1944. *They were executed according to the order given by Waldheim* in retaliation for desertion from the German army of some other persons . . . [my italics]

There was no reason for Committee I to change Mayer's testimony since the Yugoslavs did not submit any documents to support the claim that Waldheim gave an order for the murder of hostages at Sarajevo. Indeed, Waldheim could not have authorized the killings. According to David Kahn, the author of *Hitler's Spies*, the definitive study of German military intelligence, it is not possible that a junior intelligence officer like Waldheim could have given the order to execute prisoners.[1] Contrary to press reports Waldheim was basically little more than a clerk with no command powers. Thus on every count the testimony of the German prisoner Johann Mayer has no credibility.

The statement against Waldheim of the POW Klaus Melinschoff was also changed by the UNWCC. In the Yugoslav *Odluka* Melinschoff testified, 'It is possible that in Army Group E they acted on the basis of the highest orders.' This was changed by Committee I in Waldheim's UNWCC dossier to a statement by Melinschoff that 'measures of reprisal and retaliation were applied by the German General Staff and high-ranking German officers. The same line of action was taken by the accused.' In the *Odluka* Melinschoff described Waldheim as the 'aide-de-camp and assistant' of Lieutenant Colonel Warnstorff. Waldheim's supposed guilt was to have been the result of his association with Warnstorff, the head of the Ic/AO. But if Waldheim is a war criminal his superior Warnstorff should be even more guilty. But the Yugoslavs have never listed Warnstorff, his deputy Major Hammer or any of Waldheim's co-workers. Clearly Waldheim was the Yugoslavs' target.

There are numerous other indications that the 1947 Yugoslav *Odluka* against Kurt Waldheim is without foundation. In fact, the entire Yugoslav case against Waldheim is based on the claim that he was the 'Abwehr officer with the Ic [intelligence] staff of Army Group E'. The Yugoslav indictment claims that members of the Abwehr counter-intelligence organization participated in 'the selection of those detained as well as hostages for the preparation of retaliation'. It can be proved, however, that Waldheim had no connection with the AO-Abwehr unit in the Ic/AO group. Ironically, the World Jewish Congress themselves have proved this. They have

1. Telephone interview and letter from David Kahn.

released hundreds of pages of Waldheim's war-time documents, none of which indicates an Abwehr connection. The charge that he was a member of the Abwehr counter-espionage organization was fabricated against Waldheim by the Yugoslavs, since his position as an 03 had no connection with war crimes.

Why did the Yugoslavs single out Waldheim despite the absence of any evidence against him? And why would the UNWCC list Waldheim as a suspected war criminal on the basis of undocumented testimony from German POWs held by the Yugoslavs. To answer this last question we must consider how the UNWCC operated.

The main purpose of the Commission was to list those whom a member government might wish to extradite from the suspect's home country or any foreign nation where he might be hiding. It was hoped that no country would refuse the extradition request for a man whose case was judged substantive by a panel of international legal experts. Most of the cases submitted to the UNWCC were bona fide but how many is not clear.

This was true of Yugoslav cases, many of which were based on documents conclusively showing that the accused ordered or executed war crimes. This was possible because, as the official history of the War Crimes Commission notes, the Yugoslav indictments were 'based chiefly on captured archives'.[1] Indeed, Tito's army captured huge quantities of Axis records including many of the files of the Italian 2nd Army and German Army Group E. These records were thoroughly examined by the Yugoslav National War Crimes Office (which obviously could find no documents incriminating Kurt Waldheim). Clearly the Yugoslavs used the

1. *History of the United Nations War Crimes Commission*, p. 484.

undocumented testimony of German POWs because they lacked any real documentation against Waldheim.

The problem with the UNWCC is that it did not require member governments to present solid evidence. Many cases were placed on the roster of suspected war criminals despite the lack of documentation. According to a surviving member of the UNWCC, Dr Herbert Mayr-Harting, the task of Committee I was 'only to decide whether a prima facie case existed. The function was not a judicial one.[1] In reality, cases were rejected only if the papers were not in order. The UNWCC official history states: 'It cannot be too firmly emphasized that in the final analysis the value of the work of Committee I was almost wholly dependent upon the good faith of the member governments in submitting bona fide cases based on adequate evidence.'[2] And adds that 'without exception the member governments kept that faith'. But in point of fact there was no check to see if this was true. The UNWCC did not require that the actual documents be submitted but only a 'description of evidence available'. In the case of Kurt Waldheim there were no documents but only the statements of the German POWs which the committee rewrote to accentuate the guilt of the accused. It is no wonder that Shavko Odic, a member of Yugoslav State Security who participated in the 1947 attempted blackmailing of Waldheim, told the *Washington Post* that the *Odluka* prepared against Waldheim didn't amount to much: 'All that evidence, all that testimony is by and large useless.'[3]

The Commission clearly made no attempt to verify that the testimony of POWs was freely given. A country such as Yugoslavia would not have permitted international experts to

1. WB, p. 249.
2. *History of the United Nations War Crimes Commission*, p. 484.
3. *Washington Post*, 30 October 1986. For evidence that many other UNWCC files were prepared for political purposes, see pages 86–8.

check the conditions under which German POWs were being held. Thus there was no way to stop Yugoslavia or any other member of the UNWCC from submitting a bogus war crimes case based on the undocumented testimony of POWs. No representatives of the London-based War Crimes Commission ever interviewed Mayer or Melinschoff. Nor did Committee I consider whether it was possible for Waldheim to give orders for war crimes. Under the circumstances the inclusion of Waldheim's name on the UNWCC list proves nothing.

It has been suggested that the listing of Waldheim by the US Army-controlled Central Registry of War Criminals and Security Suspects (CROWCASS) is an indication of guilt. But documents in my possession make it clear that names were placed on the CROWCASS registry without any independent investigation by the US Army.[1] The purpose of the CROWCASS wanted list was to help various governments which may have wished to locate a suspect who was being held in a detention camp in Germany. The mere fact that Waldheim was listed by the UNWCC was enough to get him on the CROWCASS wanted list. The Yugoslavs informed the Allied authorities that they needed help to apprehend Waldheim because he was 'on the run', but documents published in Yugoslavia indicate that the Belgrade government knew that Waldheim was in Vienna 'employed as secretary in the [Austrian] Foreign Office.[2]

Indeed it was his position in 1947 as secretary and confidential aide to the Austrian Foreign Minister Karl Gruber that earned Waldheim a place on Yugoslavia's list submitted to the UNWCC. As we shall see in Chapter IV, there is overwhelming evidence that Waldheim was a target of blackmail

---

1. APO 742 Army 'What is CROWCASS?', December 1946.
2. *Vecernje Novosti* (Belgrade), 26 March 1986.

which is why the Belgrade government fabricated the case against him.

The Yugoslavs made a major effort to get Waldheim listed by the UNWCC. The Yugoslav mission in London was instructed by Dusan Nedeljkovic, head of the Belgrade National War Crimes Office to give 'particular attention' to Waldheim's case.[1] This despite the inclusion of many major war criminals on the Yugoslav list submitted to the UNWCC including Konrad Schubert, chief Nazi political officer in the German embassy in Zagreb. There is no legal reason why a staff lieutenant like Waldheim should have been given priority over high officials who really made policy and gave the orders.

The fact that Tito was more interested in using the UNWCC list for blackmail than for prosecuting Nazis should not be surprising. The Belgrade government frequently subordinated war crimes investigations to political considerations when it accused domestic opponents and dissidents of being collaborators and war criminals.[2] Many people recently interviewed in Yugoslavia indicate that dozens of other Germans and Austrians besides Waldheim were placed on the UNWCC list because the Belgrade government wished to blackmail them.

Waldheim has repeatedly stated that the accusations against him in the 1947 Yugoslav dossier are totally unsubstantiated. He has correctly pointed out that when Mayer and Melinschoff signed their statements they, like thousands of other Wehrmacht POWs in Yugoslavia, had 'a rope around their necks'. There was a storm of protest when Waldheim stated that 'there were atrocities on both sides' in the brutal anti-partisan war, but this also is true. Of course the Austrian

1. *Vecernje Novosti* (Belgrade), 29 March 1986.
2. A British report notes that Tito's government 'insisted on treating all Yugoslavs who were out of sympathy with the present regime as war criminals and traitors': PRO: 371/6670/U271.

President is greatly impeded in his defence since he cannot admit that he was blackmailed by the Yugoslav government. But his assertion that the UNWCC file proves nothing is correct.

Since March 1986, an intense effort has been made to convince the public that Kurt Waldheim is a war criminal. The promoters of this campaign seek to use Waldheim's military record to discredit a man who served as UN Secretary General at a time when the General Assembly passed the famous 1975 resolution condemning Zionism as a form of racism. The campaign against Waldheim has been supported by Yugoslavs who wish to advertise the extensive war crimes committed by the Nazis in the Second World War Balkan theatre. The news media have widely publicized the Waldheim war record in its pursuit of 'a good story'.

The height of this publicity was reached in the spring of 1986, during the Austrian presidential election. Some of the stories carried by the American television networks reflected base sensationalism, for example the appearance of Holocaust survivors claiming that Waldheim looked like an SS officer they remembered seeing at Auschwitz. The use of death camp survivors to gain rating points is clearly reprehensible.

Some of the newspaper and magazine stories on Waldheim have reflected a substantially distorted image of his war-time importance. In one British magazine article a Yugoslav writer claimed that the young lieutenant 'had the power to command even regular army colonels in the field.[1] The WJC have implied that the intelligence section of the Army Group E staff where Waldheim worked had considerable influence in policy-making, including the decision to launch reprisals, massacres and other atrocities. But if the Ic section was

1. Moncilo Selic, 'Waldheim's Tito connection', *New Leader*, 16 June 1986.

responsible for so many atrocities it seems odd indeed that Lieutenant Colonel Herbert Warnstorff, the section chief, survived the war but was not listed by the Yugoslavs on either the UNWCC or CROWCASS lists. The truth is that Warnstorff returned to private life after the war whereas Waldheim obtained a sensitive position in the Austrian Foreign Office which made him an ideal target for blackmail. Had Waldheim returned to private life he probably would not have been listed by the Yugoslavs.

Second World War German military doctrine relegated intelligence officers to a very low level of status and influence. Unlike the staffs of other armies, which had large and important intelligence sections working to gather information on the enemy, the Wehrmacht believed that since it was the best army in the world it had no need to worry about what the enemy might do. German commanders were expected to act decisively, forcing the other side to react to Wehrmacht initiatives. The real power on a German army staff lay in the operations section whose senior officer together with the chief of staff and the army group commander were the real policy makers.

David Kahn's *Hitler's Spies* is considered the definitive study of German military intelligence. Kahn points out that since the Germans had 'a disdain for intelligence', the chief of intelligence in an army group high command (such as Waldheim's chief, Lieutenant Colonel Herbert Warnstorff) at a staff conference 'usually spoke [only] when spoken to.'[1] If Warnstorff, the chief of the intelligence section, had such a low status, what possible policy-making role could have been exercised by an assistant adjutant like Lieutenant Kurt Waldheim? Over the years Waldheim has told many lies but describing his role on the army group staff as 'just a sort of clerk' isn't one of them.

Waldheim's subordinates included perhaps two or three

1. Kahn, *Hitler's Spies*, p. 407.

men. As an 03 (military intelligence officer) his chief responsibility was to evaluate intelligence on the enemy. Waldheim had absolutely no command powers. Among his tasks was drawing maps and making reports. According to the 1 December, 1943 organization chart (document 4), Waldheim and First Lieutenant Helmuth Polizia were responsible for 'maintenance of the mail registry book for confidential matters', 'evaluation of enemy situation' and 'activity reports'. The Ic/AO organization sheet assigns intelligence on Greece and the surrounding area to First Lieutenant Krohne, while Polizia was responsible for intelligence dealing with all non-Balkan countries including Great Britain.

The June 1986 WJC report (p. 34) claims that Waldheim was responsible for *Sonderaufgaben* – described as 'secret measures related to mass terror, torture or executions'. But the Ic/AO organization chart indicates that First Lieutenant Krohne was responsible for *Sonderaufgaben*. Military historians, including Professor Manfred Messerschmidt of the Federal Research Institute for Military History in Freiburg, concur with contemporary witnesses that *Sonderaufgaben* correctly refers to 'other duties including interpreting, courier and liaisons'. The misinterpretation of *Sonderaufgaben* is just one more example of the WJC and their former consultant, Dr Robert Herzstein, making unsubstantiated accusations against the former UN Secretary General.

The WJC have also accused Waldheim of involvement in interrogating prisoners. Lieutenants Krohne and Polizia were responsible for *Gefangenenvernehmung* – prisoner interrogation. There is reason to believe that Waldheim may have been present at POW interrogations, but David Kahn and other experts agree that the actual interrogations were not conducted by the 03, whose function was to write up reports based on the raw data obtained at the interrogations.[1] This must be kept in mind as we examine the charges that Waldheim was responsible for atrocities against Allied POWs.

Another of the WJC's endless list of accusations against Waldheim is the claim that he was responsible for 'personnel matters' of the intelligence group. Thus it is claimed that he supervised the 'political reliability' of the members of his section. On the face of it, this is bizarre since Waldheim's own 'political reliability' in the Nazi regime was under suspicion. At any rate the organization chart indicates that First Lieutenant Polizia and not Waldheim was in charge of 'personnel matters', which was not in fact political but instead referred to securing replacements for the enlisted men on the intelligence staff who were transferred or sent on leave or vacation.

Despite all these charges, Waldheim's critics have not been able to produce any evidence to refute the testimony of military historians and veterans of the Ic and hundreds of documents, all of which indicated that Waldheim's responsibilities were primarily clerical. His most important duty was to deliver to the chief of staff the morning report, which the WJC have implied was of great importance in shaping policy. However, the morning report 'basically supplied information on the events of the evening; it did not attempt evaluation'.[2]

The WJC report (pp. 34–36) gives an unrealistic view of the relationship between the young Lieutenant Kurt Waldheim and the Army Group Chief of Staff General Schmidt-Richberg. It is claimed that on 20 May 1944 when Waldheim briefed the general, 'discussed at the meeting was the use of hostages', and that at the briefing of 13 June, 'discussed at the meeting was the use of civilian slave labour'.

1. Letter from David Kahn to author.
2. Kahn, *Hitler's Spies*, p.407.

An examination of the documents cited by the WJC gives a different impression of what occurred during the briefings of 20 May and 13 June.[1] Wehrmacht generals did not 'discuss', 'confer' or 'meet' with lieutenants. In all probability, when Waldheim delivered his reports to General Schmidt-Richberg, he stood at attention. It would have been almost impossible for him to make any comment unless asked a direct question by the general. It was Schmidt-Richberg who referred to slave labour and hostages. Waldheim played no role in planning these actions and it is misleading to imply that he did.

In fact, many misleading stories have been published about Waldheim's duties. The impression has been given that Waldheim had wide-ranging power in the interrogating of POWs and their dispatch to the SD (*Sicherheitsdienst*) for execution. The Ic staff 03 actually had the task of evaluating information obtained at interrogations. The Ic section translators, not Waldheim, actually interrogated prisoners. According to the Ic/AO group organization chart, Lieutenant Colonel Warnstorff and his deputy, Major Hammer, dealt with the SD and other branches of the SS. It would be one of these two officers and not Waldheim who arranged for the transfer of Allied prisoners to the Nazi criminal organizations.

The opening sentence of one news story indicates that on 17 October 1943 Waldheim 'gave orders to the Luftwaffe to transport eleven captured British commandos' from the island of Levitha.[2] Understandably, such reports have created great concern, particularly in Britain. Of course, anyone familiar with the operation of the Wehrmacht realizes that a young staff lieutenant had no authority to order the Luftwaffe to do anything. In fact the entry in the Army Group E war

1. NA: T-311/175/0988 and 0993.
2. *New York Times*, 30 December 1986.

diary states: 'Major General Winter gave instructions to First Lieutenant Waldheim for transmittal to the Air Force that Army Group E wishes to have the prisoners on Levitha picked up by Junkers and the German occupation forces to be provided with weapons and whatever else they need.[1] Clearly, Waldheim was merely relaying a message from General Winter to the Luftwaffe which was part of his normal clerical duties. The documents in question certainly do not suggest that Waldheim had any jurisdiction over POWs.

Waldheim has created suspicion by his insistence that he 'was never involved in the handling of prisoners generally and of captured commandos in particular'. Such a claim is not quite true and once again demonstrates the ineptitude of Waldheim's defence. Clearly the former Secretary General should have given an honest indication of his limited clerical duties and responsibilities. Waldheim's total denials are exploited by the WJC, which attempt to give the impression he committed atrocities against British POWs.

The WJC report mentions a document which indicates that on 18 July 1944 the British Commando Sergeant John Dryden was handed over to the SD by the Ic/AO.[2] The fact that Waldheim initialled the document indicates that he was familiar with the transfer of Sergeant Dryden, but there is no evidence that he conducted the interrogation of the British commando or made the decision to hand him over to the SD.

However, the most embarrassing document against Waldheim is a telex he sent to the South East Command on 26 April 1944 regarding a captured British commando, which notes 'request decision on immediately sending prisoner to the Sicherheitsdienst'.[3] But there is no evidence that Waldheim sent this message on his own authority or that he

1. NA: T-311/175/756.
2. ND: NOK W-179.
3. *Epoca*, 16 October 1987.

actually handed the commando over to the SD for 'special treatment'. Indeed, after viewing all the documents the British Ministry of Defence was 'unsuccessful' in finding any evidence of criminal activity by Lieutenant Waldheim.

It should be kept in mind that commandos were in fact little more than terrorists. Commandos on both sides took no prisoners and frequently killed or injured civilians. It was common practice on both sides to execute captured commandos. Of course, the liquidation of a commando is still a war crime but morally it cannot be compared to the cold-blooded murder of Jews and other innocent civilians.

The greatest effort of the WJC and other critics of Waldheim has been aimed at finding some way to involve the former Secretary General in the Holocaust. But despite the constant claims no evidence has been produced to indicate Kurt Waldheim played any part in the removal of Jews from the Greek Islands in 1944. This initiative and all other 'political matters' were handled by Warnstorff, Hammer and the Abwehr unit.

Thus on 21 April 1944 it was Hammer who sent a message to Korpsgruppe Joannina ordering the registration of all Jews and foreigners within its command area.[1] Copies were sent to the higher SS and Police Command in Athens. There is no indication that the AO sent a copy to the Ic section. *Indeed, none of the documents dealing with the deportation of Jews was signed by or addressed to Waldheim.*

Some confusion results because communications intended for the Abwehr unit were addressed to the 'Ic/AO group'. This was a military formality since Lieutenant Colonel Warnstorff, the overall head of the Ic/AO group, reviewed all incoming communications.

There is no reason why Waldheim should have been given

1. See Document 7.

copies of communications dealing with the deportation of Jews. Waldheim has pointed out that the *Handbook for Services on the General Staff* makes it clear that the Abwehr dealt with 'political matters' while the Ic section handled only strictly military duties. Historians support Waldheim's assertion that there were orders forbidding the passing of sensitive information except on a 'need to know basis'. The Austrian President has also claimed that he was away on his various sick and study leaves when most of the deportations were carried out. While it is unlikely that he had any detailed knowledge about the deportations, it is impossible to imagine that he did not have at least a general idea about what was being done to the Jews. But of course knowledge of atrocities is not a war crime. Despite the lack of evidence the media support the WJC claims that Waldheim was involved in the Holocaust.

Newspaper reports indicate that in July 1944 Jews were deported from Crete and Rhodes 'upon instructions from the Ic/AO' intelligence group.[1] As in most stories of this type no effort is made to indicate the distinction between the Ic section and the Abwehr unit which actually dealt with the SS. The claim is made that Waldheim was the 'deputy chief intelligence officer of the section'. But in reality it was Major Hammer who was deputy chief of the group as well as AO (Abwehr Offizier) in charge of 'political matters' such as the deportation of Jews, in which Waldheim played no role.

It is unlikely that any incriminating documentation against Waldheim will ever be found. Professor Hagen Fleischer of Crete University has made an exhaustive study of the transportation of Greek Jews. He has compiled a list of all Wehrmacht officers implicated in the deportation and asserts that Waldheim was not involved. According to Fleischer,

1. *Jewish Week*, 11 July 1986.

Kurt Waldheim 'had nothing to do with Greek Jewry'.[1] And yet many self-appointed 'experts' have appeared on American television claiming that Waldheim is a war criminal because of his supposed involvement in the deportation of Greek Jews to Auschwitz.

Perhaps the most absurd charge against Waldheim concerns his alleged role in anti-Semitic propaganda. The 'evidence' is a group of leaflets prepared by a German propaganda company of the XXXIV Army Corps and sent to the AO unit. These pamphlets, which were meant to be dropped on Soviet troops, contain several anti-Semitic sentences such as 'cursed be the Jews who sit over the necks of our relatives . . . and suck their blood'.[2] Elan Steinberg of the WJC claims that the pamphlets are important since they represent 'another shocking thing he's [Waldheim's] involved in'. But this is just one more example of how the WJC have tried to discredit the former UN Secretary General.

It has been alleged that the pamphlets were sent to Waldheim but his name does not appear on the letter accompanying the booklets, which were intended for the Abwehr unit. All evidence indicates that it was the AO section which dealt in propaganda.[3] The WJC base their claim on the initials 'WAL' which appear in the AO box on the receipt for the pamphlets. If these were Waldheim's initials it would certainly implicate the former UN Secretary General not only in anti-Semitic propaganda but, more important, it would substantiate the claim that he had Abwehr duties.

In presenting the pamphlets to the press the WJC typed in 'WAL' next to the illegible initials in the AO box. However James T. Miller, an acknowledged handwriting expert, has since given a sworn statement that the initials could not

1. *New York Times*, 6 March 1986.
2. *Newsday*, 24 September 1986.
3. Document 5, second page.

have been Waldheim's. The US Justice Department has refused to accept his expert opinion despite the fact that Miller has appeared as a government witness in previous cases.[1]

Such tactics have characterized the case by the World Jewish Congress and US Justice Department against the former Secretary General but have gone unreported in the British and American press.

Much of the WJC report deals with the Stip–Kočani massacre of 114 Macedonian villagers by the Wehrmacht in October 1944. The principal 'evidence' is a statement signed by Captain Karl-Heinz Egberts-Hilker before he was executed by the Yugoslavs for leading the attack. According to the WJC the statement of Egberts-Hilker represents 'important testimonial evidence' which shows that Lieutenant Kurt Waldheim was the staff officer responsible for the raid on the three villages along the Stip–Kočani road in Macedonia. Great worldwide publicity was given to the charge that Waldheim was linked to the Stip–Kočani massacre, based on the statement of Egberts-Hilker.

The testimony of the Wehrmacht captain was mentioned in the *Odluka* submitted to the UNWCC but was not accepted by its Committee on Facts and Evidence in 1948. Eli Rosenbaum, then legal counsel of the WJC, claimed that the Committee declined to accept Egberts-Hilker's testimony only because he was about to be executed and thus would not have been available for a Waldheim trial.[2] This explanation certainly sounds plausible but there was a far more compelling reason why the UNWCC rejected Egberts-Hilker's statement. Now that the original Yugoslav *Odluka* has become

1. *Profil*, 4 May 1986.
2. Telephone interview, 15 May 1986.

available we can see the truth. In his statement Egberts-Hilker never even named or referred to Kurt Waldheim!

The Wehrmacht captain mentions only a Führer order for reprisals against civilians. In presenting Egberts-Hilker's statement to the UNWCC as evidence against Waldheim, the Yugoslav National War Crimes Commission used some rather flawed reasoning. It claimed that since reprisals were ordered by the SD and Abwehr, the command for the Stip–Kočani reprisal must have come from Waldheim who was identified as an Abwehr officer on the intelligence section of the Army Group E staff. But as we have seen Waldheim was not an Abwehr officer and had nothing to do with this counter-intelligence organization or with reprisals.

In all probability no one gave Egberts-Hilker the order to massacre the population of the three villages along the Stip-Kočani road. At his trial the Wehrmacht captain stated: 'I have always emphasized that I bear the sole responsibility ... I never attempted to pass responsibility to my superiors or claimed that I was acting under orders.[1] Clearly the WJC owe Waldheim an apology for making the claim that the testimony of Egberts-Hilker implicates him in the Stip-Kočani atrocity.

Equally erroneous is the WJC claim that they have located 'extraordinary new documentation' to support their charge that Kurt Waldheim was responsible for the Stip–Kočani massacre. These documents, which according to the WJC report (Annex, page 6) are 'devastating to Waldheim's defence', turn out to be several routine memoranda made by the young lieutenant two days before the massacre, which identify Stip-Kočani as an area of considerable partisan activity.[2] The first is the morning report of 12 October 1944, in which he noted:

1. *Profil*, 24 November 1986.
2. NA: T:311/183/630 and 636.

Macedonia: Increased partisan activity (XV Brigade) against Stip–
Kočani road. Arrival of XI Macedonian Kumanovo-Brigade from the
area of Brod into the area of Skoplje.

In a second report later in the day, Waldheim noted:

Macedonia: Further partisan forces (presumably parts of V Prilep-
Brigade) advancing towards Stip–Kočani road. In fighting between
national Albanians and parts of VI Macedonia and XII Communist Zrna
Nava-Brigade west of Kumanovo substantial enemy losses, among them
113 dead.

As any competent expert will testify, these documents do
not in the least suggest criminal activity. Waldheim makes no
recommendation for reprisals or atrocities nor does he even
urge a German attack in the area. In view of the low priority
given to intelligence by the Germans it is far from certain that
such routine reports made by a junior intelligence officer
were even read by anyone in authority on the High Command
of Army Group E. It is ludicrous to pretend that these
documents prove anything. Unfortunately the news media
gave wide publicity to the story of Waldheim's involvement in
the Stip–Kočani massacre since they adopt the WJC attitude
that papers signed or initialled by Waldheim must have some
sinister significance.

Other documents released by the WJC show that reports of
atrocities did pass through the intelligence section of Army
Group E's staff. Undoubtedly Waldheim was aware of the
widespread brutal practices of Army Group E. But this knowledge does not constitute a war crime. What is conspicuously
missing is any documentation showing that Waldheim
ordered atrocities or even recommended reprisals. It is
claimed that 'Waldheim became officer 03, an expert in the
art of organizing reprisals'.[1] However, given Waldheim's low
status on the staff of Army Group E there is no reason to

1. Rosenzweig and Cohen, *Waldheim*, p. 83.

believe he had the authority to make such recommendations. David Kahn indicates that an 03 definitely could not order reprisals and it is unlikely that he could even recommend them.[1] None of the documents produced by the WJC contradicts this expert opinion.

Another erroneous charge against Waldheim is the claim that he played a role in rounding up and deporting Italian POWs after Italy's defection from the Axis alliance in September 1943. Some newspaper reports tried to give the impression that the transportation of Italian POWs was somehow equivalent to the deportation of Jews to Auschwitz. But the shipment of Italian POWs to detention camps in Germany was a military necessity. Italy's capitulation created a critical situation for Army Group E since the Germans had to disarm and round up the Italians before they and their arms went over to the Greek and Yugoslav partisans, thus rendering the position of the Wehrmacht in the Balkans impossible. It is the generally recognized right of a belligerent to move against an ally which has surrendered.

When France defected from its alliance with Britain in 1940, Churchill ordered swift action to neutralize the French army and navy, which led to the death of some French servicemen. It is of course true that many of the Italians were badly mistreated when they arrived in Germany but there is no evidence that Waldheim was involved in this.

The idea that the former Secretary General played a role in the deportation of Italian soldiers from Greece is based on the transcript of a phone conversation between Waldheim and Lieutenant Frey, an assistant adjutant at Army Group E headquarters at Arsakli.[2] Waldheim merely reported that 1,300 Italian officers and nearly 24,000 enlisted men, now

1. Letter to author.
2. Document 8.

POWs, were being transported from the Peloponnese to Athens. There is no mention of any mistreatment.

Professor Robert Herzstein of the University of South Carolina, a former consultant to the WJC, has claimed that Waldheim 'was responsible for the deportation of more than 25,000 Italian non-coms and enlisted men. He did it personally.'[1] This and similar statements by various people affiliated to the World Jewish Congress are seriously misleading.

First, the Italians mentioned in the transcript were not being deported but simply shipped from the Peloponnese to Athens. More important, it is totally absurd to imply that an assistant adjutant like Waldheim was personally responsible. In his conversation with Frey, Waldheim was not giving orders but reporting on events decided by others. Besides it is debatable whether the transportation of POWs was a war crime. Of course, Waldheim's critics want to give the impression that since the former Secretary General was 'linked' to the transportation of Italian POWs he must be involved in the deportation of Jews.

It is clear that the World Jewish Congress have uncovered no evidence to support the bogus war crimes charges brought against Waldheim by the Yugoslavs in 1947 for the purpose of blackmail. In an interview Eli Rosenbaum, then the legal counsel of the WJC, conceded that 'there is no case for murder against Waldheim'. He indicated that the WJC hoped to make a case against Waldheim for something called 'incitement to murder'. Rosenbaum claimed that such a charge had been used before but he could cite no precedent.[2] Rosenbaum's comment amounted to a *de facto* admission that there was no legal case against Waldheim. It is no wonder that the war crimes expert Simon Wiesenthal has criticized the WJC

1. *Southern Israelite*, 7 November 1986.
2. Telephone interview. On 15 May 1986 Rosenbaum told the *New York Times* that Waldheim could be charged with 'complicity in murder'.

and described Waldheim as 'an opportunist but not a war criminal'.[1]

Since the Austrian election in June 1986 there has been a periodic effort to revive the war crimes charges against Waldheim. One of the most notable occurred on 30 October 1986 when Dusko Doder published two articles on Waldheim in the *Washington Post*. One dealt with the blackmailing of Waldheim by the Soviet and Yugoslavs, and had a great deal of useful information, as we shall see in Chapter IV.

It is, however, Doder's other article, dealing with the Kozara massacre, which attracted the greatest media attention. It is not surprising that the Serbian-American journalist would focus on the slaughter of Serbian civilians by Axis forces at Kozara in the summer of 1942. There is no doubt that this was a major war crime, which Doder described in considerable detail. However, the claims on the American TV networks that the *Washington Post* article contains significant new information linking Waldheim to the Kozara massacre are baseless. Doder's revelations about Kozara were neither new nor particularly significant. In Vienna a spokesman for the Austrian President told the *Washington Post* correspondent that Waldheim had served with the West Bosnian Combat Group in the Kozara area as a supply officer around the time of the massacres. Doder also mentioned a medal which Waldheim received from the Nazi puppet Croatian government after the Kozara campaign.

As with so many other aspects of the Waldheim story, his receipt of the Croatian Zwonimir medal on 22 July 1942 has been the subject of serious misinformation. Most decorations given out in war are simply morale boosters signifying nothing. This is particularly true of those exchanged between

1. *New York Times*, 17 May 1986. For more on Wiesenthal see pages 153–4.

the Wehrmacht and its allies. The Germans and Italians showered medals on each other to promote 'Axis solidarity'. Croatia, an Axis puppet state, was generous indeed in its distribution of the Zwonimir medal to its German comrades in arms.

Kurt Waldheim's Zwonimir award was number 916, indicating that 915 had been distributed in the six months since its inception. Clearly a high percentage of Axis officers fighting on the Croatian front had received the Zwonimir decoration. In fact, German personnel clerks simply sent in lists of men on their rosters including numerous non-combatant personnel. High-ranking German officers and those who distinguished themselves in combat with the West Bosnian Combat Group received more significant decor-ations than the Zwonimir medal, such as the Croatian Dreiblatt.

The Zwonimir decoration included a citation for 'courag-eous conduct in the fighting', but this was a meaningless phrase added to bolster the importance of an insignificant award. Indeed, the list of those decorated the same day as Kurt Waldheim includes a medical doctor and a paymaster – hardly combat and war crimes types.[1] Waldheim's position as a supply officer with the West Bosnian Combat Group during the Kozara campaign was equally innocuous, but it has been portrayed in the most sinister light by his critics and the press.

Waldheim's revelation to the *Washington Post* that he had been in the Kozara area in the summer of 1942 had been previously mentioned in the 2 June 1986 WJC report and even earlier in the press. Waldheim has vacillated several times over whether he was at Kozara around the time of the campaign, claiming that both his memory and his records are deficient. However, Waldheim was not compelled to admit

1. Document 9.

that he had been an assistant adjutant serving as an aide to Captain Plume, the quartermaster of the West Bosnian Combat Group during the Kozara campaign. There are no documents indicating his position at the time. The former UN Secretary General's critics have used his revelation that he was in the quartermaster branch to create a scenario in which he theoretically could have committed war crimes while serving with the West Bosnian Combat Group.

According to a 2 June 1942 document signed by Colonel Muckel, the quartermaster for the German command in Belgrade, prisoner deportations were among the duties of the quartermaster branch of the West Bosnian Combat Group, which was instructed that 'anticipated arrival date and number [of prisoners] are to be reported by phone before each transport leaves'.[1] The Justice Department 'secret report' contains a staff memorandum of 13 July 1942 from the West Bosnian Combat Group indicating the 'beginning of prisoner transport to transit camp Belgrade-Semlin'.[2] This constitutes the total documentation for Waldheim's supposed role in the deportation of prisoners after Kozara – which is generally considered the strongest charge against him. It isn't much. In fact, it is nothing.

Even Dusko Doder in his article of 7 November 1986 admits: 'The documents do not mention Waldheim and there is no evidence that he was personally involved in the deportations.' The former UN Secretary General has produced a witness, the supply clerk Ernst Wiesinger, who has testified that Waldheim was in the quartermaster branch but had no involvement with prisoner transports. These were handled by an 'Einsatzkommando' unit in the West Bosnian Combat Group, which included another supply officer and railway

1. *Washington Post*, 7 November 1986.
2. *Profil*, 25 May 1987.

officer. There is no documentation to contradict this testimony. Indeed, the only evidence that points to Waldheim's role at Kozara is his own testimony and that of his witness. It is hard to believe that Waldheim would be so foolish as to volunteer that he was in the quartermaster branch of the West Bosnian Combat Group if he had been involved in prisoner deportations. OSI has ignored not only Wiesinger's testimony but also a document indicating that the duties of the IB02, the position held by Waldheim, were limited to organizing supplies and keeping the war diary of the quartermaster department.

An Austrian Foreign Ministry document issued at the time of Waldheim's retirement in 1983 showed that he listed the Zwonimir medal in his personal file. Had Waldheim done anything criminal at Kozara, he would not have been so open about a decoration he received as a result of the campaign.

While there is no evidence that Waldheim committed war crimes at Kozara, his explanation of his role in the campaign suffers from his inept defence. Not only has he changed his story several times but, even worse, he told a journalist that at Kozara 'there was no massacre, there were fierce battles'. Understandably, such a remark outraged the entire Yugoslav population.

On 27 April 1987 President Kurt Waldheim of Austria was placed on the Attorney-General's 'watch list' of aliens barred from entering the USA. To put Waldheim on the list, the Justice Department had to establish that he had 'assisted or otherwise participated in the persecution of persons because of race, religion, national origin or political opinion'.[1] This law has usually been applied to former members of the Gestapo, SS or other criminal Nazi organizations which the

1. *New York Times*, 28 April 1987.

Justice Department wished to exclude from the USA. Clearly this law should not be used to bar the head of a friendly country who was an ordinary soldier in the Wehrmacht unless there was evidence against him that would stand up in court.

At Nuremberg, people against whom much stronger cases were made were acquitted of all involvement in war crimes. Indeed, if Waldheim had not been the target of the most powerful political lobby in Washington, there would be no question of placing him on the 'watch list' since there is not a single shred of evidence that has the slightest chance of being used against him in a court of law. Most other heads of state around the world are far more guilty than Waldheim of having 'assisted or otherwise participated in the persecution of persons because of race, religion, national origin or political opinion'.

The Justice Department's case against Waldheim is contained in a 200-page secret report. Although most of it has been leaked to the press, not even Waldheim or members of the Austrian government have been officially permitted to see it. A report on Klaus Barbie prepared by OSI was immediately published despite the fact that it contained many sensitive revelations of the relations between the 'Butcher of Lyons' and American intelligence. The Waldheim report deals exclusively with his war-time service.

The use of the 'secret report' has turned Waldheim into a Dreyfus in Austria. Even in the USA many have asked questions. On 27 May 1987 the *New York Post* demanded in an editorial: 'Let the Justice Department set out before the public the evidence on which the Attorney-General's "watch list" decision was based.' Of course the *New York Post* assumed that there was some new evidence which links Waldheim to war crimes, but this is not the case. According to the *New York Times*, the case against the Austrian President 'does not depend on any new information uncovered in the last year'.[1] For the most part, the Justice Department memorandum is based on the WJC report of 2 June 1986, together with some 'evidence' obtained in Yugoslavia.

At a briefing on 27 April 1987 the Justice Department spokesman presented the usual allegations against Waldheim, including charges that he took part in 'reprisals and executions of hostages' and that he turned over 'Allied prisoners to the SS'. Waldheim was also accused of being involved in deporting Greek Jews as well as 'the use of anti-Semitic propaganda'.[2] As we have seen there is no evidence that Waldheim was responsible for deportations or turning prisoners over to the SS. It is hard to believe that the Justice Department would attempt to resurrect the totally discredited 1947 Yugoslav charges that Waldheim ordered the execution of hostages. Everyone involved in the Waldheim case knows that the dossier submitted to the UNWCC is based on totally fraudulent undocumented statements coerced from prisoners of war for purposes of blackmail. Indeed, experts consulted by the *Washington Post* characterized the 1947 Yugoslav indictment against Waldheim as 'useless' and 'legally unpersuasive'.[3] The charge that Waldheim was responsible for the propaganda pamphlets which have his initials typed in is more of an embarrassment to the WJC than Waldheim.

The Justice Department report also contains 'new evidence' which OSI obtained in Yugoslavia in December 1986. This concerns Waldheim's service in 1942 when he acted as liaison with the Italians and later as a member of the quartermaster branch of the West Bosnian Combat Group during the campaign at Kozara. These documents from 1942 have been floating around Yugoslavia for some time. I first learned about them in September 1986 when I visited

1. *New York Times*, 29 April 1987.
2. *New York Times*, 28 April 1987; *New York Daily News*, 29 April 1987.
3. *Washington Post*, 30 October 1986.

Yugoslavia and met people who had copies of them and wished to gain my assistance in view of my knowledge of Italian military records. I was reluctant to co-operate since it was clear that the German documents from the Yugoslav archives proved nothing against Waldheim. According to press reports these documents show that while Waldheim 'was acting as liaison with *Pusteria* division', Axis officers planned war crimes. It is also alleged that Waldheim 'worked in villages where Jews were deported' and that the quartermaster branch was 'processing prisoners for deportations and execution in the Kozara action'.[1]

We have seen that there is no evidence Waldheim was involved in the deportation. His name isn't even mentioned in any of the documents from the quartermaster branch of the West Bosnian Combat Group dealing with deportations. The other allegations in the OSI report are equally far-fetched.

In May 1942, 500 prisoners of the *Pusteria* division were handed over to the SS for slave labour while Kurt Waldheim was liaison to the Italian unit. This transaction is recorded in the *Pusteria* war diary but there is no mention of Waldheim's name. None the less, the Americans claim that since Waldheim was a 'channel of information' he must have been involved.[2] Once again, we see the Justice Department's 'presumption of guilt' which has so characterized its case against Waldheim. Ironically, even if the OSI could prove that Waldheim translated at meetings where deportations were planned, such a purely mechanical function would not be a war crime.

The third allegation refers to the deportation of Jews to Jasenovic concentration camp from Banja Luka on 31 July 1942 while Waldheim was stationed in the town. There are

1. *New York Times*, 29 April 1987.
2. *Profil*, 25 May 1987.

no documents indicating Waldheim's involvement but OSI simply assumes that since Waldheim was probably in the town when the deportations took place he must be involved. Waldheim claims that he was not in the Banja Luka area on that date. Besides, there is evidence that the deportations were carried out by the Ustashi, a criminal Croatian organization which specialized in the extermination of Jews and Serbs living on Croatian territory.[1]

In view of the speculative nature of the accusations against the former UN Secretary General it is no surprise that the Justice Department is so reluctant to make public its report on the Waldheim case. If the OSI or the WJC had a single document indicating Waldheim's guilt, it would not be kept secret but would immediately be published on the front page of every newspaper in America and Europe. The Justice Department has not even been able to come up with a plausible explanation for keeping the Waldheim report secret.[2]

The OSI report does not begin to make a case against Waldheim for 'being connected with' or acting as an accomplice in war crimes. People against whom a far stronger case was made have been acquitted of having even an indirect role in war crimes. For example, in 1947 SS Colonel Josef Vogt was charged by the prosecutors at Nuremberg with being an accessory. Vogt was a high-ranking official in the bureaucracy which administered concentration camps. In its verdict on Vogt the Nuremberg Tribunal held that 'the phrase "being connected with" a crime means something more than having knowledge, it means something more than being in the same building or even in the same organization'.[3] In the light of the Tribunal's acquittal of Vogt, there can be no question of any

1. Herve Lauriere, *Assassin au Nom de Dieu.*
2. For more on the OSI's secret report see pages 164–9.
3. *United States War Crimes Trial*, Vol. 5, Case 4.

case against Waldheim on even the most minimal war crimes charge.

The fact that Waldheim was stationed in a district or town where Jews were rounded up does not constitute evidence that he participated in the deportations. And even if the Justice Department can show that some of the men in the quartermaster corps of the West Bosnian Combat Group helped process prisoners for execution, this does not prove that Waldheim was among them. Clearly all the evidence supports Waldheim's assertion that his duties concerned the handling of supplies for the West Bosnian Combat Group. Nor does Waldheim's position as a translator implicate him in war crimes. Hitler's interpreter, Paul Schmidt, was never charged with war crimes. The Nuremberg Tribunal specifically exempted from prosecution all technical and clerical employees who performed purely mechanical functions. Obviously the German documents from the Yugoslav archives prove nothing. This should not be surprising. If the German archives captured by the Yugoslavs after the Second World War had contained material implicating Waldheim, the documents would surely have been used in the 1947 indictment instead of the false, undocumented testimony of German POWs in the *Odluka*.

After a massive search by several teams of investigators in half a dozen countries, not a single document implicating Kurt Waldheim in war crimes has been uncovered. To commit war crimes it is necessary for a soldier to serve in the field where he comes into contact with his victims or he must be in a policy-making staff position. Waldheim never served in the field in the Balkan theatre. His staff assignments were all extremely unimpressive.

Service in the Ic intelligence section and the quartermaster branch were hardly choice assignments in the Wehrmacht, while liaison with the Italians was probably the most despised job in the German Army. Throughout the Balkan campaign, Waldheim received but one promotion, finishing the war with the rank of only first lieutenant. He was not a general staff officer nor was he offered a regular commission. This was a remarkably dismal record for a man with five years' war-time experience and a doctorate from the University of Vienna. With his background Waldheim should have been given a job of importance, such as in the operations section, or command of his own unit with the rank of captain or major. Obviously Waldheim was never fully trusted, perhaps because of his father's anti-Nazi background and his own tendency to speak out against the Nazi regime.

Some have conceded that although there is no document- ation indicating that Waldheim is a war criminal, he is 'mor- ally guilty' because he knew about atrocities. On 15 May 1987 a delegation from the Justice Department met Austrian officials to discuss the Waldheim case. According to press reports, 'the American delegation brought no new historical documents that directly implicated the Austrian President in war crimes'.[1] Incredibly, the Justice Department team informed the Austrians that Waldheim had been placed on the 'watch list' principally because he was 'in a position to know about war crimes in the Balkans'.

In point of fact every American who served in Vietnam, every Israeli in Lebanon and every Russian in Afghanistan had knowledge of atrocities against civilians, but no one has ever suggested that every man who served in these brutal campaigns is a war criminal. Clearly the Department's case against Waldheim is a sham. Placing a man like Waldheim on the watch list for political considerations discredits the efforts to pursue genuine war criminals.

As the cases of Klaus Barbie and Josef Mengele demons-

1. *New York Times*, 17 May 1987.

trate, there is still a need to keep open the possibility of prosecuting genuine war criminals whose atrocities are such that there should be no statute of limitations on their apprehension. However, the trial of former SS men, concentration camp guards, and Gestapo officers may come to an end because this matter has been so completely politicized.

CHAPTER III

The London Commission

Since March 1986 when it was revealed that the records of the United Nations War Crimes Commission contained a dossier on former UN Secretary General Kurt Waldheim, considerable attention has been focused on the UNWCC files, which the UN is now finally making available to member governments. While the World Jewish Congress has agitated over the former Secretary General's war service, the Israeli government has carried on an effort to embarrass the UN by demanding that the UNWCC files be opened to the general public (see pages 156–64). In their zeal to support the Israeli initiative the American news media, particularly the major New York newspapers, have conveniently ignored the Jewish state's own role in covering up the UNWCC files for several decades. Also being overlooked is the evidence that Kurt Waldheim's file was not the only false UNWCC dossier prepared for political purposes.

During the years of its existence in the 1940s the UNWCC considered 40,000 cases submitted by seventeen member governments. It is probably true that most of these people were involved in war crimes. However, the procedures of the Commission left much to be desired. As F. F. Garner of the British Foreign Office war crimes section noted, 'When examining cases brought before it the Commission only hears one side of the case.'[1] He feared that many of the charges might be 'groundless'. Somewhat later Garner wrote 'we have reason to believe that many of the cases submitted to the Commission (especially those submitted by countries in the

1. PRO: FO 371/66570, 1 January 1947 memorandum.

Slav group) are based on political considerations rather than purely legal principles'.[1] The Foreign Office was not alone in this evaluation of the UNWCC. The British embassy in Washington notified the war crimes section that the Americans 'entirely agree with our attitude and are most unhappy about the political use to which the Commission is being put'.[2]

The Polish were under suspicion of having listed some people with the UNWCC for political purposes. Indeed the UNWCC files became a useful tool in the deepening Cold War. The Greeks also improperly used the UNWCC. As a Foreign Office memorandum noted, 'The Commission recently listed General Marinov, the Bulgarian Minister in Paris, on charges brought by Greece. However, it now appears that the case was trumped up by the Greeks in order to discredit the Bulgarian delegation at the Paris Peace Conference.'[3]

The worst offenders, however, were the Yugoslavs. Indeed, the American occupation authorities did not recognize the validity of the listing of former Wehrmacht personnel by Yugoslavia with the UNWCC. According to a Foreign Office memorandum, 'United States military authorities in Germany and Austria have been forced to insist that applications for the surrender of alleged war criminals made by Yugoslavia should be supported by full evidence irrespective of whether the persons concerned have been listed by the Commission.'[4] It is ludicrous that in 1987 the Justice Department should bar the Austrian President from entry into the USA because of a case based largely on a forty-year-old undocumented UNWCC file which the US

1. Ibid, 7 June 1947 minute.
2. Ibid, 19 June 1947 letter.
3. Ibid, 1 January 1947 memorandum.
4. Ibid, 9 June 1947 memorandum.

occupation authorities in Austria in 1947 considered at best to be suspect.

The British and Americans recognized the validity of Wehrmacht documents presented by the Belgrade government since, as we have seen, a large part of the archives of Army Group E was captured by the Yugoslavs. Unfortunately, however, the UNWCC did not require that the actual documents indicating war crimes be presented to its Committee on Facts and Evidence but only a 'description of evidence available'.[1] Thus a country such as Yugoslavia which wished to present a phoney case to the UNWCC could either describe nonexistent documents or give a false description of available material or, as in the Waldheim case, submit the undocumented testimony of prisoners of war held in concentration camps.

It should be stressed, however, that the majority of UNWCC cases, including those listed by Yugoslavia, were undoubtedly bona fide. The Germans with their Italian and Croatian allies committed enormous atrocities in Yugoslavia. While suspicious of some of the cases, the British did not consider all the UNWCC files to be false. According to a memorandum by Patrick Dean of the Foreign Office:

It is agreed that the investigation and listing activities of the UNWCC should come to an end soon; this would *not* mean that the existing records would be disposed or destroyed and it would be very important that these should be kept in existence so that they would be available until the persons named upon them have been tracked down and trials have taken place whenever the necessary evidence can be obtained.[2]

F. F. Garner, head of the war crimes section of the Foreign Office, believed he knew what should be done with the UNWCC files. He wrote: 'On the face of it, it seems quite a

1. UNA: record group 30 registration sheet, p. 1.
2. PRO: FO 371/66570, 2 January 1947 memorandum.

good idea that the UN should take over those functions of the UN War Crimes Commission which will remain when the Commission is wound up.'[1] On 15 December 1947 Colonel George A. Ledingham, chief secretary of the Commission, was contacted about the files by UN Secretary General Trygve Lie, who wrote: 'This question might be discussed between the competent officials of the two organizations with a view to determining conditions of transfer.'[2]

On 30 August 1948 Bertil Renborg, the chief UN archivist, drew up rules governing access to the UNWCC files which were designated as UN record group 30. Renborg proposed that certain portions of the UNWCC files be restricted, including 'the list of war criminals, suspects and witnesses and related indexes and the formal and related papers' or any document which refers to specific individuals. According to the archivist the restricted papers should be made available 'for official United Nations purposes' as well as 'upon official written request of member states of the United Nations'.[3] These rules would have meant that any member state of the world organization could gain automatic access to the classified portion of the record group 30 files simply by presenting a written request. It was understood that the restricted sections of the UNWCC files would not be available to the press, historians or the general public, in order to protect people who had not been put on trial.

As suggested by Secretary General Trygve Lie, the UN archivist Renborg submitted a copy of his proposed rules governing access to the war crimes files for the approval of the UNWCC chairman Lord Wright, and its legal counsel Dr J. J. Litawski. In a report of 3 October 1949 Renborg noted that Wright and Litawski 'have expressed satisfaction with the

---

1. Ibid, 4 February 1947 minute.
2. UNA: record group 30, box 5, misc. 118.
3. UNA: CRF (Central Registry File) Renborg to Pelt, 30 August 1948.

proposed rules and neither has suggested any change'.[1]

However, as has been mentioned, without referring to Lord Wright and Dr Litawski, in 1949 the Assistant Secretary General for Legal Affairs, Ivan Kerno, changed the rules effectively barring access to member governments. As early as 1947 the Foreign Office noted with regard to the UN taking over the work of the UNWCC, that Kerno 'does not seem to be co-operative'.[2] On 2 November 1949 Kerno criticized the rules drawn up by Renborg which had been approved by Lord Wright and Dr Litawski, the two highest officials of the War Crimes Commission. According to Kerno, 'the most important question raised by the proposals it seems to me is whether the secret and "confidential" material containing charges relating to specific individuals should be made available to member governments simply upon request'. Kerno proposed that the UNWCC files be used 'only for official United Nations purposes'.[3] This rule which barred member states from consulting the restricted portions of the UNWCC files was never approved by the leaders of the War Crimes Commission or the General Assembly but remained official UN policy for over three decades (until March 1986 when the UN announced that the record group 30 files would be available to member governments but not the general public).

There is no evidence to suggest that Kerno was acting on other than his own legal judgement. However, the policy he initiated of keeping the record group 30 case files closed to member governments, and thus barring the use of UNWCC material to prosecutors, must surely have had the approval of the nations most directly concerned, including the USA,

1. UNA: CRF Renborg to Pelt, 3 October 1949. Renborg later wrote to Litawski: 'I am most pleased that you felt that the proposed rules are satisfactory.': Renborg to Litawski, 5 October 1949.
2. PRO: FO 371/66570, 11 February 1947 minute.
3. UNA: CRF, 9 November 1949, memorandum.

Great Britain and the Soviet Union, and at some point Israel. It is no accident that record group 30 was never raised as an issue at the UN even by the Soviets in their frequent attacks on the world organization. Obviously all governments concerned realized that it would be embarrrassing to pursue people employed on both sides of the Iron Curtain and to expose the political plots which motivated many of the blackmail attempts.

There have been many exaggerated claims about the contents of the restricted portion of the UNWCC files. The Israeli ambassador to the UN called record group 30 'a treasure trove of new information'.[1] As mentioned, the files in the UN archives contain only a brief summary of the evidence against each suspect. The real documentation is included in the complete files which are held by each of the seventeen member governments. Any prosecutor who wishes to obtain evidence to use in a war crimes case would certainly wish to go directly to the governments concerned to obtain the relevant documentation. Of course, in some cases the complete file held in government archives may not amount to very much. Kurt Waldheim's file in the Yugoslav archives consists only of the undocumented testimony of German POWs.

The UNWCC charge files of 40,000 German, Japanese, Italian, Hungarian, Bulgarian and Albanian accused persons are contained in 125 boxes stored in the UN archives.[2] The largest groups are the French and Polish cases against Germans. There are also a very substantial number of Yugoslav charge files. It will probably never be known how many of these cases are phoney. In view of the documentary evidence and the testimony of veterans of the Yugoslav security service (which we shall consider in the next chapter) scores, perhaps

1. *New York Times*, 25 March 1987.
2. See Document 10.

even several hundred, Germans and Austrians were placed on the UNWCC files for political purposes. There are probably many other cases which have simply been poorly researched. There are people in the charge sheets of every country who are not war criminals. The UNWCC files can be a useful research tool for serious prosecutors but it is a source that must be used with caution by journalists and historians.

Very few people listed by the War Crimes Commission were ever prosecuted. The UNWCC and CROWCASS were part of a system set up during the Second World War to deal with the war crimes problem. Conspicuously missing from this system was any provision for a police force actually to apprehend the suspects. Nor was there any systematic effort to deal with members of the SS or other groups which committed the worst atrocities. In the pre-computer age the UNWCC, and particularly CROWCASS, suffered from bureaucratic inefficiency due to their small inexperienced staffs.

The major problems developed, however, as a result of the Cold War. The Soviet Union never joined the UNWCC or CROWCASS, ostensibly due to a dispute over Russian demands that the puppet Baltic states be included as members to compensate for the membership of the British Dominions. There was also, of course, the previously mentioned tendency for many member states to use the UNWCC and CROWCASS for political purposes by listing those they wanted to embarrass or blackmail.

As the Cold War developed the Western powers were anxious to close down the War Crimes Commission since they saw no reason to antagonize the Germans and Italians whom they wished to gain as allies. The former Nazi and Fascist war criminals appeared more and more as reliable anti-Communist allies. It seemed to the Anglo-Americans that Italy and West Germany would be ungovernable if a vigorous prosecution of former Nazis and Fascists were carried out. After the United Kingdom and United States had prosecuted those Germans, Italians and Japanese guilty of crimes against British and American POWs, there seemed little reason for the Western powers to continue with the UNWCC.

The UNWCC files were safely hidden away in the UN archives where they would remain until I discovered this document collection in 1979. But the War Crimes Commission had distributed hundreds of copies of the list of 40,000 names which it had declassified.[1] All the member governments had received copies, including the United States and Great Britain. The Soviets were also supplied with a copy of the list. In May 1986 a copy of the UNWCC list #156 was found on the open shelf in the US National Archives. Numerous other copies have been found in various government departments.

As has been seen, Simon Wiesenthal knew about the list. Serge Klarsfeld, the Nazi-hunter who tracked Klaus Barbie to South America, had access to the UNWCC register.[2] Indeed, Tom Bower in his 1982 book on the cover-up of Nazi war criminals after the Second World War actually reproduces a page of the UNWCC list which he apparently obtained in the Public Record Office in London.[3]

The official story is that Waldheim's UNWCC file was not known to any foreign governments. But with so many copies

1. On 8 June 1948 the US Department of State notified the American mission in Budapest that 'the Department is informed by the Secretary General of the [UN War Crimes] Commission that all its lists including those originally classified as Very Secret or Secret are now unclassified': WRNC: RG 8-1948-711.

2. A 1983 book about Klaus Barbie notes that the Gestapo murderer 'figured on the 239th place on the first war crime list established by the United Nations'. He gives as his source an interview with Serge Klarsfeld: Brendan Murphy, *The Butcher of Lyon*, p. 221.

3. Tom Bower, *Blind Eye to Murder*.

of the UNWCC register distributed, the US Justice Department's OSI was surely not the only war crimes investigation unit which made a computer search of the list. It is not known how many other people on the register were the subject of blackmail.

For three decades the UN carried on a classic cover-up of record group 30. The UN information office was instructed to tell callers that the UNWCC files were not located anywhere in the UN system. Written inquiries from war crimes investigators in several countries, including West Germany and Brazil, were answered with a variety of stories including the assertion that the files could not be located. More often the Secretariat admitted that they had the files but refused to grant access, claiming 'the restrictions now in effect were based on the policies of the UNWCC and on a desire to protect the individuals and governments concerned'. The UN legal office was in error when it asserted that its rule barring access to member governments had been 'approved by Lord Wright and Dr J. J. Litawski'.[1]

In 1960, however, there was an agreement between the UN and Israel whereby the latter obtained the record group 30 files on Adolf Eichmann. Since the Nazi butcher had never worked for the West German government, NATO, the CIA or any Communist government, no objections were raised to Israel's request for Eichmann's files. But the Secretariat had to find a legal justification for giving Israel what had been denied on other occasions. It is of some interest that in the correspondence related to the release of Eichmann's UNWCC files there is the following admission by Oscar Schacter of the UN legal office:

The original draft of the rules provided that the restricted records could be inspected upon official written request of a member state and thus was

1. UNA: CRF, 4 March, 1953 memorandum.

agreeable to the chairman and legal officer of the war crime commission. On November 2, 1949, however, the Assistant Secretary General in charge of the legal department recommended the present wording.[1]

It is clear that Israel knew about the UNWCC files since at least 1960, but did nothing to obtain access to these records for war crimes prosecutors. In 1980 Ambassador Rosenne told me that Israel made a 'gentleman's agreement' in which it acquiesced in the cover-up of the 40,000 war crime dossiers after receiving the files on Eichmann. In fact, with the exception of the Eichmann and the recent Demjanjuk trials, Israel has done remarkably little to pursue genuine war criminals. Many well-informed sources indicate that as part of a deal to get reparation payments from West Germany in the 1950s the Zionist state agreed to avoid war crimes investigations. Morris Schappes, editor of *Jewish Currents*, notes 'the agreement between Adenauer and Israel on reparations involved playing down anti-Nazism'. According to Milton Friedman of the Jewish Telegraph Service, when 'Israel made a deal to get reparations a tacit deal to cool down war crimes complaints' was made.[2]

But West Germany has made its own effort to pursue at least some Nazis. In the spring of 1986 the UN Secretariat announced that the secret portion of the UNWCC file would be open to member governments but not yet to journalists or historians. The UN legal office claimed that this had always been its policy but this is refuted by the documents. There is some hope that the UNWCC files might be put to good use in West Germany. The war crimes document centre at Ludwigsburg, West Germany added five full-time investigators to its staff when the United Nations War Crimes Commission files became available.[3] Ludwigsburg has a good

1. UNA: CRF, letter from Oscar Schacter to Stoper-Bobsek, 5 August 1960.
2. Rocelle G. Saidel, *The Outraged Conscience*, pp. 24–25.
3. *New York Times*, 14 May 1987.

record in prosecuting Nazis but a great deal remains to be done. The UNWCC files which are now available to the Bonn government contain dossiers on a number of people living in West Germany.

Hans Ernst (UNWCC file France A31/203) was the Gestapo chief in Angers, France. Several years ago a case against him in West Germany was dropped for lack of evidence. It would of course be interesting to see if the information in his UNWCC file might help to revive his case. Fritz Merdesche (France A80/497) was the Gestapo chief of Orleans where he is accused of having organized a massacre of Jews in 1944. Otto Kumm (Yugo A-1/698) was in 1943 the commander of the Prinz Eugene SS division. In recent years he has helped establish the SS veterans' association. Kumm has been an outspoken defender of the SS; thus there are many who would like a careful examination of his record.

Some of the suspected war criminals listed by the UNWCC have been active in the West German government. Heinrich Illers (France S62/417), a Gestapo official in Paris, was the president of a court in Saxony under the Bonn government. V. Odewald (France S62/6900) worked in the Office for the Protection of the Constitution in Lower Saxony in the 1960s. There are of course hundreds of people listed by the UNWCC who are alive in West Germany, many of them former Bonn government employees. Perhaps action may yet be taken against them.

There is little cause to be optimistic that the UNWCC files will now be used for legitimate war crimes investigations. Like all aspects of the war crimes story the history of the UN War Crimes Commission has been marred by political intrigue. From the beginning all governments involved have subordinated the pursuit and prosecution of war criminals to other considerations. It should not surprise anyone familiar with the history of war crimes investigations that many people were listed with the UNWCC so that they could be black-mailed. Nor should it be surprising that forty years later Israel would use the UNWCC files as a means of embarrassing the UN while ignoring the thousands of genuine war criminals named on the list. Kurt Waldheim's name on the UNWCC list has not been ignored. There can be no doubt, however, that in 1947 the young diplomat was among those placed in the UNWCC for political purposes. Indeed Waldheim's war crimes file must be seen for what it is – no more or less than a relic of the Cold War.

CHAPTER IV

A Relic of the Cold War

By April 1945, the situation of Army Group E was desperate. General Löhr was conducting a fighting withdrawal, hotly pursued by Tito's partisan army, which was not only liberating their country but had an eye to the annexation of Carinthia, an Austrian border province with a partly Slav population. In view of the deteriorating military developments, assistant adjutant Kurt Waldheim was ordered to join an infantry division in the Trieste area.

In these last weeks of the war there was no longer a direct travel connection between Army Group E headquarters in Zagreb and Waldheim's assignment in Trieste so that he tried to get to his new post via Klagenfurt, the provincial capital of Carinthia. Waldheim claims that amidst the disintegration he was unable to reach his new unit, thus he headed back home to join his wife and newly born daughter.

With the cessation of hostilities in May 1945, US occupation authorities sent Waldheim to Bad Tolz camp in Bavaria for interrogation. On 26 April 1945, US intelligence reports mentioned Waldheim so they apparently knew about him and his position.[1] Waldheim was of great interest to American intelligence.

The use of former German intelligence officers proved to be consistent with US policy after the war. A prime example was General Reinhard Gehlen, the German army's senior intelligence officer on Soviet matters ... In June 1945 Gehlen met with Major General

1. The reports were made by the predecessor of the CIA, the Office of Strategic Services (OSS) – telephone interview with CIA press officer.

William J Donovan, chief of the Office of Strategic Services and OSS European Chief Allen Dulles.[1]

During this period intelligence about Communist Yugoslavia was perhaps as highly prized as information about the Soviet Union.

After the Second World War there was serious danger of a clash between the Western powers and the Yugoslav partisan army which was sweeping into Carinthia. President Truman backed Churchill's determination to oppose with force the annexation of Carinthia by Communist Yugoslavia. Many in Washington and London believed that a good thrashing delivered to Tito would be a useful lesson to Stalin not to attempt the seizure of any more territory in Central Europe. Churchill alerted General Sir Harold Alexander, the Allied commander, who replied: 'My soldiers will obey orders but I doubt whether they will fight against Tito with as much enthusiasm as they did against the hated Germans.'[2] War was eventually avoided but the British and Americans remained poised for a clash with Yugoslavia, a country about which they knew little.

Kurt Waldheim was a gift for US intelligence. Most of the Army Group E intelligence staff had been captured by the Yugoslavs. As an 03, Waldheim had a wealth of information about a country which the Western Allies might have to invade at any moment. Waldheim had supervised making maps so that he knew the best invasion routes and where Tito was likely to make a stand. He was familiar with the composition and organization of the Yugoslav military forces as well as their top personnel. There is also reason to believe that he knew about Tito's treasonable negotiations with the Germans which the Western Allies could have used as a political

1. Murphy p. 229.
2. Lucas, *The Last Days of the Reich*, p. 129.

weapon to destroy the Yugoslav dictator's credibility.

Waldheim, who was reliably anti-Communist, had never joined the Nazi party and during the war had served in staff positions removed from any atrocities. With his educational background, wealth of useful information and correct political attitude, Waldheim was a man the Americans found very useful indeed. Thus began his long association with US intelligence.

After his interrogation at Bad Tolz, Waldheim was sent to Vienna where he was hired for the Austrian Foreign Office by its First Secretary Fritz Molden, who in 1948 would become the son-in-law of Allen Dulles, the European chief of the OSS and future director of the CIA. During the war, Molden, scion of a distinguished Austrian family, had been recruited by Dulles for the OSS. He had established a formidable network of contacts throughout Eastern Europe which would serve the Americans in the Cold War. Molden assigned the former intelligence officer, who lacked any diplomatic experience, to what Waldheim called 'not just a job, it was *the* job' as private secretary to Karl Gruber, the Austrian Foreign Minister. Waldheim revealed that Gruber also had 'clandestine links to Allen Dulles, the long-time head of the CIA'.[1] There is also evidence that Gruber worked for British intelligence. Located in the old Habsburg Ballhausplatz, the Foreign Office under Gruber and Molden became a centre of Western influence in the Vienna government that ruled a divided country. This was the period of 'Four men in a jeep' when Austria was occupied by Soviet, American, British and French forces. Vienna was also the scene of considerable Cold War tension and intrigue which has been caught so brilliantly by Graham Greene in *The Third Man*.

1. Waldheim, *In the Eye of the Storm*, p. 22.

Gruber has admitted that it was 'probable' that Molden 'kept up his contacts with American intelligence' while he worked as First Secretary at the Ballhausplatz. Gruber explained: 'It may be his father-in-law said, "Work a little for me." He obviously was trusted by American sources.' Gruber added that one of the reasons he had chosen Molden as First Secretary is because 'he had good standing with the Americans'.[1] Gruber himself was also involved with Allen Dulles, who had recruited the Austrian resistance leader as an agent during the war.

When asked if Kurt Waldheim had a relationship with American intelligence during this period, Gruber reluctantly conceded 'it's quite possible he did'. It seems hard to believe that people like Gruber and Molden would have recruited a man like Kurt Waldheim into their inner circle, with access to all their private papers, unless the former Wehrmacht officer had come to some understanding with American intelligence while he was being interrogated at Bad Tolz. This would have been no more than the usual procedure during this period.

Of course, if Waldheim had had a suspicious past, US intelligence would not have sent him to the Vienna Foreign Office to work in such a visible position for Gruber and Molden. American intelligence sometimes recruited people with a criminal background but they were placed out of sight. On a 5 November 1945 application form Kurt Waldheim listed his membership in the SA riding corps and his service in the Balkans during the war.[2] Presumably Gruber and Molden understood the difference between joining the riding club and membership of the Nazi party. They surely also realized the distinction between an 03 in military intelligence and an Abwehr officer. Molden probably appreciated

1. *New York Times*, 25 April 1986.
2. See Document 11.

Waldheim's association with Professor Verdross, who had been a member of the POEN/05 anti-Nazi resistance movement in which Molden had served. Most important, Waldheim possessed the same type of conservative anti-Nazi and anti-Communist attitude of Gruber and Molden. There is no question of anti-Nazi resistance leaders like Gruber and Molden ever having hired anyone with a Nazi or war crimes background.

Fritz Molden noted the check he conducted on Waldheim's background when he joined the Foreign Ministry:

Based on the good contacts to the American authorities in Vienna resulting from my war-time activities as liaison between the Austrian resistance – POEN/05 – and the Allies, I also established contact with the CIC (counter-intelligence corps) and the OSS (office of strategic services), the predecessor of the CIA, and concerned them with this issue ... Both authorities eventually told me that, based on their research, there were not the least charges against Dr Waldheim with respect to any Nazi past.[1]

The CIC was of course quite familiar with Waldheim's background from his interrogation at Bad Tolz. There was no reason to give him anything but a good reference since his name did not appear on any list of members of Nazi criminal organizations.[2]

In early 1946 there was an anonymous denunciation of Waldheim accusing him of having a Nazi past. The Foreign Ministry conducted another investigation. Waldheim submitted statements from the mayor of his home town, Tülin, as

1. WB, p. 131.
2. Since Waldheim was investigated by two US intelligence agencies it is impossible to believe that a CIA official was being honest when he wrote to Congressman Solarz in 1980 that his records showed that after Waldheim was wounded in Russia 'he was discharged from military duties following his recovery and returned to study law in Vienna': Hillel Seidman, *United Nations: Perfidy and Perversion*, p. 149.

well as local Socialist and Conservative party leaders, all of whom confirmed the anti-Nazi attitude of Kurt Waldheim and his family. Waldheim pointed out the non-political nature of his activities in the SA riding corps. Gruber recalls: 'Minister of Interior Helmer told me that there is no reason to object to Waldheim.'[1] Indeed, all Austrian officials had to be cleared by an Allied de-Nazification commission but there is no record of any objection being made to Waldheim. Obviously if a position such as assistant adjutant in the intelligence branch had been considered criminal, it would have been impossible to find people to serve in the post-war Austrian government.

In his memoirs Waldheim boasts of his close relations with Foreign Minister Gruber. 'I was in no way a protégé of his but a real friendship developed.'[2]

Gruber supposedly told a colleague, 'If someone else tells me we can't do anything about a problem, I won't believe him. But if Waldheim says it I know that he would explore every avenue to solve a problem or do something about it. Therefore, if he comes and says it is impossible, I believe it.' Obviously, the twenty-eight-year-old fledgeling diplomat had found the type of influence he had lacked in the Wehrmacht. However, his prominent position was noticed by the enemies of the pro-Western Austrian Foreign Office.

All serious researchers working on Waldheim agree that his UNWCC file was prepared against him for purposes of blackmail. This is obvious from documents attached to the *Odluka* as well as the testimony of former members of the Yugoslav secret police which makes it clear that Waldheim was one of the many people against whom a war crimes dossier was fabricated for political reasons. This story has

1. *New York Times*, 4 March, 1986. *Profil*, 3 March, 1986.
2. Waldheim, *In the Eye of the Storm*, p. 22.

surfaced despite the efforts of the Belgrade government to conceal it.

In 1947 Waldheim's superior, Austrian Foreign Minister Karl Gruber, was a thorn in the side of both the Soviets and their reluctant satellite Yugoslavia. The Russians resented Gruber's tendency to make the Ballhausplatz into a centre for Western influence in Vienna. The Yugoslavs were concerned by Gruber's denial of reparation payments but especially his refusal to make border rectifications in Carinthia. This boundary dispute was being discussed at a four-power conference in London which greatly concerned the Tito government. The Yugoslavs tried to find some embarrassing information on Gruber's past but as a former leader of the Austrian anti-Nazi resistance he proved invulnerable. The Yugoslavs also investigated the background of Hans Piesch, the provincial governor of Carinthia, who was also included in the Austrian delegation to the London conference. The Yugoslavs claimed that Piesch had a 'Nazi record'. The matter was investigated by the Allied Control Commission in Vienna which found that Piesch had been deprived of his job in 1938 'for having refused to sign a declaration of loyalty to the Nazi party'.[1] But despite the fact that he was cleared of all charges Piesch was very soon replaced as governor of Carinthia with a man more acceptable to Vienna. The incident may well have impressed the young Waldheim with the idea that even those who are cleared of bogus Nazi charges face dismissal, since the Western powers wished to avoid a diplomatic incident. This helped explain why Waldheim feared even bogus war crimes charges.

After the effort to embarrass the Austrians with Hans Piesch, Yugoslav interest next turned to Gruber's trusted aide, Kurt Waldheim. On 12 December 1947 Uros Bjelic of

1. PRO: FO371-64046.

the legal office of the Belgrade Ministry of Interior sent a message to the Yugoslav Ministry of Foreign Affairs.

Waldheim ... is today in Austria and not only as a free person but as a Secretary in the Ministry of Foreign Affairs (Legation Secretary). He is a member of the delegation of the Austrian Foreign Minister, Dr Gruber, and was with him in London. This fact is also of no minor importance for the Foreign Ministry. We submit this information in view of its possible relevance to the activities of Austrian Foreign Minister Dr Gruber against our national interests.

Inform us if an *Odluka* should be prepared on Gruber's assistant, Waldheim, which will result in his being registered with the UN War Crimes Commission.[1]

The decision was taken to register Waldheim with the UNWCC. On 18 December 1947 Dusan Nedeljkovic, president of the Yugoslav National War Crimes Commission notified the Yugoslav embassy in London: 'You should first of all make efforts to register Waldheim, the reason being that the evidence is good and the indictment is fully sufficient, but also because from another point of view it is especially useful politically.'[2] On 26 December 1947 Nedeljkovic wrote to the Yugoslav Foreign Ministry telling them that Waldheim's *Odluka* had been sent to the UN War Crimes Commission in London 'with mention of the specific importance of the registration'.[3] Nedeljkovic also reminded the Belgrade Foreign Office that Waldheim 'is a member of the entourage of Austrian Foreign Minister Dr Gruber'. Clearly the man the Yugoslavs were after was not Waldheim but Gruber.

About this time Anton Kolendic, a Yugoslav security agent, and his deputy, Vasilije Kovacevic, received a list of twenty-five or thirty names and the files of former Wehrmacht soldiers who had been placed on the UNWCC register for

1. Document 12A.
2. *Washington Post*, 30 October 1986.
3. Document 12B.

political purposes. Kolendic recalled: 'Waldheim's name was fourth on the list and was underlined. He was described as an official of the Austrian Foreign Ministry.'[1] Kolendic's aide, Kovacevic, had collaborated with Mustafe Golubic, a Soviet agent who proposed that the Russians might be able to use the list, which was given to Colonel Gonda of the Red Army.[2]

According to Kolendic, in 1947 Soviet intelligence began to recruit people in large numbers:

At that point they realized the weakness of the Austrian Communists. Their political position was eroding rapidly although they were still in the government. But the Russians figured that they could not count on this situation to continue for a long time and therefore began approaching people from the bourgeois parties. They could recruit people by say, facilitating the return of your son from a Soviet POW camp or by giving food or other favours or by blackmail. They were particularly angry with Gruber, whom they considered to be a British agent, not merely a British sympathizer but an agent. I heard Gonda and other Soviet officers including generals talk about an incident that could be staged to eliminate Gruber. Hence their interest in Waldheim, who was Gruber's secretary, working in Gruber's office. Don't forget these were Stalin's intelligence agents.[3]

A plan was concocted to force Gruber to resign at a meeting of the four-power council by 'exposing' his aide, Kurt Waldheim, with a phoney UNWCC dossier. Fortunately for Waldheim he was transferred to Paris before the scheme was carried out.[4] But Kolendic is 'absolutely certain' that Waldheim was recruited by the Soviets. The former security agent believes that Waldheim 'must have been terrified' when he was approached by the Soviets. At the height of the Cold War Vienna was the centre of espionage and intrigue, and assassinations and kidnappings were common occurrences.

1. *Washington Post*, 30 October 1986.
2. *Duga* (Yugoslav magazine), May 1986.
3. *Washington Post*, 30 October 1986.
4. *Profil*, 13 July 1987.

Kolendic, who has recently been under great pressure from the Yugoslav government, has been forthcoming about the Soviet effort to blackmail Waldheim, but he is understandably reluctant to admit that the Yugoslav government had also used Waldheim's *Odluka* for its own political purposes.[1]

Another former Yugoslav intelligence agent who served as an aide to Slobodan Penezic, deputy to Alexander Rankovic, the secret police chief, indicated that the Yugoslavs were interested in Waldheim. 'Rankovic decided that we should try to recruit him,' he recalled. 'That was not difficult in those days. You showed your victim the document but then you tell him everything would be fine, you'd protect him provided he would do something for you in return. And that was in 1947. You had to feel the atmosphere of that year. War crimes trials were still going on. People were afraid.'[2] The former intelligence aide claimed to have seen a memorandum Kolendic sent to Belgrade about his discussion with Waldheim and the Soviet agent Gonda. Another former Yugoslav agent indicated, however, that the Soviets let the Yugoslavs know that 'Waldheim was recruited and the Yugoslavs should stop their interference'.

Several other former Yugoslav agents revealed to Dusko Doder that in early 1948 the Soviets told Tito's security forces to lay off Waldheim. But soon after began the split between the USSR and Yugoslavia which became final in June 1949 when the Soviets dropped their support of Tito's claims to Carinthia.[3] This ended any chance Yugoslavia had of ever securing a part of the Austrian border province. However, Tito's security agents did not lose interest in

1. Kolendic has recanted his testimony to Dusko Doder of the *Washington Post*, but while in Yugoslavia I received independent confirmation of his story which was first published in a Yugoslav magazine.

2. *Washington Post*, 30 October 1986.

3. Alvin Rubenstein, *Yugoslavia and the Non-Aligned World*, p. 13.

Gruber's young aide who was obviously destined for the highest posts in the Austrian Foreign Ministry.

In the late 1940s the future Yugoslav Prime Minister, Mitja Ribicic, was deputy chief of Slovenian intelligence when he took an interest in Kurt Waldheim. Thus began a relationship that would last for four decades. Ribicic became the Yugoslav liaison with Waldheim acting on behalf of Tito as the Austrian diplomat rose in the Vienna hierarchy. Waldheim also had contacts with Ribicic, as representative of the Slovenian Catholic separatist movement which was to play a key role in the Waldheim story.[1]

After the split between Tito and Stalin, Kurt Waldheim found himself at the centre of the espionage conflict which was waged by Soviet, Western and Yugoslav agents in Cold War Vienna. We now know that the Western powers won this struggle when their Operation Silver penetrated the Soviet spy ring in Austria. During this operation the British and Americans obtained access to all Soviet communications dealing with the Balkans particularly Stalin's plans *vis-à-vis* his delinquent satellite, Marshal Tito of Yugoslavia.[2] If they had not already known about Waldheim's possible contact with Soviet intelligence, the Western allies certainly learned about it during Operation Silver.

There is no reason to doubt that Waldheim favoured Western intelligence agencies. He may have met Soviet agents but this was not so unusual in Vienna during a period when many diplomats were double and triple agents. Kurt Waldheim was an opportunist but it is hard to conceive that he would prefer the Soviets over Gruber, Molden and the Western intelligence agencies which had treated him so well. Everything we know about Waldheim suggests that he either favoured the

1. Private information.
2. David C. Martin, *Wilderness of Mirrors*, pp. 74–77.

West or was a man lost in intrigue, with no clear loyalty. Such is often the fate of a diplomat in a small neutral country.

While not spectacular, Waldheim's rise in the Austrian diplomatic service was steady. In 1948 he was appointed to the number two post at the Austrian mission in Paris. Several years later he became head of the Ballhausplatz personnel office. Waldheim's former chief, Karl Gruber, was forced to resign as Foreign Minister when he wrote a book which claimed that the Austrian government had conceded too much to the Communists. Gruber was appointed ambassador to Washington, where with his excellent contacts he was able to play a key role in the preparation of the Austrian State Treaty of 1955 which ended the four-power occupation of the country. The 1955 agreement stipulated that Austria had to remain neutral, thus rendering the country an outpost in Central Europe, caught between the NATO and Warsaw Pact forces. Waldheim notes that it was called a 'state treaty' because 'As far as we were concerned a peace treaty was not appropriate. Austria had not declared war on anyone. It had been a victim of Hitler.'[1] This type of thinking was typical of Austrians, most of whom felt that a real de-Nazification would be too divisive in view of the isolated position of the country.

As a neutral, Austria, like Sweden, played an active role in the United Nations. During most of the 1950s and 1960s Waldheim headed the Austrian delegation to the UN. The future Secretary General served as ambassador when the UN went through a dramatic shift as the General Assembly changed complexion from a pawn of the United States into a chamber dominated by the Third World. Waldheim cultivated the friendship of all factions in the UN, which paved the way for his eventual election as Secretary General.

1. Waldheim, *In the Eye of the Storm*, p. 24.

In 1968 Waldheim was recalled to Vienna where he became Foreign Minister. This soon proved to be a bigger challenge than anyone had imagined when Soviet troops invaded Austria's Communist neighbour, Czechoslovakia. As in 1956 during the Hungarian rebellion against Soviet rule, neutral Austria was placed in a delicate position.

The crisis had begun when the Czech Communist party under Alexander Dubcek launched an ambitious reform programme. But the 'Prague Spring' was short lived. The Russians feared that liberalization might take root in other satellites and perhaps the Soviet Union itself. On 21 August 1968 USSR military forces as well as those of the Warsaw Pact allies, Poland, East Germany, Bulgaria and Hungary, occupied key positions in Czechoslovakia, particularly Prague. The Czech military forces offered no opposition and there was little bloodshed compared to the brutal repression of the Hungarian revolution.

In 1956 waves of refugees had poured into Austria from Hungary. As in most countries around the world in 1968, there was considerable sympathy in Austria for their Czech neighbours. The Austrian press roundly condemned the Soviet armed intervention on a small peaceful state which was making a genuine effort to reconcile democracy with Socialism.

The World Jewish Congress and others have criticized Waldheim's role during the 1968 Czech crisis. In particular, the WJC have focused attention on a cable sent by Foreign Minister Waldheim to the Austrian embassy in Prague directing that they turn away Czech citizens seeking refuge. The 21 August cable stated: 'Please have legation building closed and allow admittance only to Austrian passport holders ... Czech citizens already found in the building should be convinced to leave the building through kind insistence with reference to the fact that the legation must be reserved for our

Nationalſozialiſtiſche ⊛ Deutſche Arbeiterpartei

Gauleitung Niederdonau G..........

‎5 /.. 1940
‎{ :. ....

Perſonalamt

Abteilung: Politiſche Beurteilung

An den
Oberlandesgerichtspräsident,

Vertraulich!

Unſer Zeichen u. Zahl
in der Antwort
unbedingt anführen!

W i e n , I . ,Justizpalast

Unter Zeichen: Pe-Sch./C.   Ihr Zeichen:
             32327   P.A. 89/40
Betrifft: Politiſche Beurteilung

Wien, den   2. August   1940
LX. Waſagaſſe 10, Fernruf A 19-5-60 bis 67
Briefanſchrift: Wien LX, Poſtamt 66, Poſtſchließfach; 199

Name: W a l d h e i m   Kurt

Geburtszeit: 21. 12. 1918   Ort: Wördern.

Wohnort: Tulln,   Straße: Wildgasse 10

Der Genannte war,wie sein Vater,ein Anhänger des Schuschnigg Regim
und hat in der Systemzeit durch Angeberei seine Gehässigkeit zu
unserer Bewegung unter Beweis gestellt.

Der Genannte ist nun zum Militärdienst eingezogen und soll sich al
Soldat der deutschen Wehrmacht bewährt haben,sodass die Zulassung
zum Justizdienst von mir nicht abgelehnt wird.

                    H e i l   H i t l e r   !
                 Der Leiter des Gaupersonalamtes:

Document 1: The August 1940 Gauleiter Report on Kurt Waldheim.

Aktenzeichen des RJM.: 1 p —

1. Vor- und Zuname: (akademischer Grad)	Dr. Kurt Waldheim Dipl.cons.Akad.
2. Geburtstag und -ort:	21.12.1918,St.Andrä-Wördern
3. Deutschblütige Abstammung: (wodurch nachgewiesen ?)	ja,durch Ahnenpaß
4. Glaubensbekenntnis:	röm.kath.
5. Beruf des Vaters:	Bezirksschulinspektor i.R.
6. Vermögensverhältnisse des Beamten:	kein Vermögen
7. Frühere Zugehörigkeit (mit genauer Zeitangabe) a) zu politischen Parteien:	./.
b) zu politischen Verbänden:	./.
c) zu Freimaurerlogen: (mit Angabe des Grades)	./.
d) zu politischen oder konfessionellen Beamten- vereinen:	./.
8. Zugehörigkeit (mit genauer Zeitangabe) a) zur NSDAP. (Mitgliedsnummer, Amt ?) b) zu einer Gliederung: (Dienstrang und Führerstelle ?)	SA.Reiterstandarte 5/90 SA-Mann seit 18.11.1938 NS.Studentenbund seit 1.4.1938
c) zu einem angeschlossenen Verband: (Amt ?)	
d) zum NS-Fliegerkorps, NS- Reichskriegerbund, Reichs- kolonialbund, Reichsluft- schutzbund, DRK., All- gemeinen der Deutschen Studenten und sonstigen Verbänden, soweit die Zu- gehörigkeit zu den Personal- akten anzuzeigen ist: (Amt ?)	

Verband Nr. 188. Personalbogen Quart

Document 2: Waldheim's 1940 application for a court position.
Waldheim mentioned his membership in the Nazi Student Union and
SA Cavalry Corps but had to leave many blanks since his Nazi
affiliations were so sparse.

GENERALMAJOR STAHL

MAJOR i. G. GEHM

OBERSTARZT Dr. WEBER

MAJOR FUNKE

MAJOR HERBST

HAUPTMANN PLUME

HAUPTMANN KONOPATZKI

KRIEGSGERICHTSRAT Dr. MAIERHÖFER

KRIEGSVERWALTUNGSRAT PATZSCHKE

STABSZAHLMEISTER MEYER

OBERLEUTNANT URBACH

OBERLEUTNANT STRNAD

OBERLEUTNANT SAUER

OBERLEUTNANT Dr. WURIANEK

OBERLEUTNANT KITTEL

OBERLEUTNANT DEEPEN

OBERLEUTNANT KREUZPAINTNER

OBERZAHLMEISTER BLEIDISTEL

HEERESJUSTIZINSPEKTOR POLASEK

LEUTNANT HÄHNEL

LEUTNANT LIPPERT

LEUTNANT HEIL

LEUTNANT BUMB

LEUTNANT LOCKEMANN

LEUTNANT WALDHEIM

LEUTNANT BÖTTCHER

ASSISTENZARZT Dr. ENGELBERG

KRIEGSPFARRER BRAUN

SONDERFÜHRER (Z) MATERN

MINISTER TURINA

MAJOR i. G. BESTALL

RITTMEISTER GOVEDIĆ

OBERLEUTNANT RITTER ULLISPERGER v. DONAUTRAU

LEUTNANT z. See VESELINOVIĆ

Document 3: The West Bosnian Combat Group 'commemorative list'. The news media has suggested that this is a roster of combat personnel who fought at Kozara. In reality it is simply a list of officers assigned to a central administrative staff that includes medical doctors, a chaplain, a legal officer, a paymaster and several supply officers, of which Kurt Waldheim was one.

Translator Lieutenant Kurt Waldheim with his superior, Colonel Hans
Macholz and an Italian General. Standing to the side is SS General
Artur Phelps. No connection has ever been established between
Waldheim and Phelps or the SS. (See page 47.)

Abteilung
Leiter: Major i.G. Warnstorff   Gruppe Ic/AO   Vertreter: Major Hammer A.O

Gruppe Ic	O 3	O 5	Ic/L
Maj.i.G.Warnstorff	Oberleutnant Waldheim	Oberleutnant Kießling	Oberleutnant Niemann Becha!
Vertr.: Maj.Hammer	Oberleutnant Polizu	Dolmetscher-Offz.	Obfeldw.Bunz

V.b. Briefingsbuch
Feindlage

Ic- Morgen- u.Abendmeldung

Feindlagebeurteilung

Tätigkeitsberichte

a) Griechenland und Randgebiete
(Bearb.:Oblt.Krohne)
Griechenland

Bulgarien, ...

Sonderaufgaben

Gefangenenvernehmung

b) Feindlage der Alliierten
(Bearb.:Oblt.Polizu)

Großbritannien

U.S.A.

Frankreich

Afrika

Mittlerer Osten

Ferner Osten

Außenpolitische Fragen

Auswertung der Ergebnisse der Rundfunkempfangszentrale

Gefangenenvernehmung

Personalangelegenheiten der Gruppe Ic/AO

Ord.Offz.z.b.V.des Ic

V.S.-Brieftagebuch

Personalangelegenheiten der Gruppe Ic/AO u.d.Abw.Tr.

Besondere Aufträge auf dem Arbeitsgebiet Ic/AO

Bearbeitung der feindlichen Luftlage und Auswertung der Luftaufklärungsmeldungen

Bearbeitung der Seelage auf Grund der Luftaufklärungsergebnisse

Übermittlung von Aufklärungswünschen an Luftwaffe

Bearbeitung der gegen Feindlage u. fremden Heere

Feindlageberichte, Feindlagebeurteilungen

Vorschlagsentwürfe für Befehle (Feindbild)

Taktische Angelegenheiten

Zusammenarbeit mit Abwehr,Geh.Fpol., Feldgendarmerie (vgl. Seite 19)

Orientierung der Verbündeten über Feind u.Feindverhältnisse im Rahmen des vom OKH genehmigten Umfanges

Disziplinarangelegenheiten für Offz. u.Mannsch.der Abwehr Tps und GFP 621

Tägliche und einmalige Meldungen der Abwehr Truppe u.

Noch Gruppe Ic/AO

Arbeitsgebiete, auf denen die Gruppe Ic/AO dem Chef d.Gen.Stabes unmittelbar untersteht.

AO	Sachbearbeiter AO	Offz.f.national-sozial. Führung (NS-Führungsoffz.)	Propaganda
Major Hammer	Sdf.(Z) Schlenker, Kdt.	Hptm. Pfitzer	Chef Prop.Kp.690
Vertr.:Oberltn.AO Hi.AO	AO	1. Zensuroffizier	

Sicherung des gesamten Nachrichtennetzes im Bereich H.Gr.E

Führung der GFP-Gruppe

Ordnung und inneres Gefüge der Truppe

Verfügungsrecht für eigene Propaganda u. Maßnahmen zur Gegenpropaganda an Prop.Kp.690 und Prop.Kp.Kreta

Meldungen an Offz.für national-sozial.Führung und Zensuroffiziere

Abwehrmäßige Betreuung u.Überwachung des Stabes H.Gr.E und der dem H.Gr.E unmittelbar unterstehenden Dienststellen

Einsatz der Feldpostprüfstelle und Auswertung der Ergebnisse

Überwachung des Grenzverkehrs, Paß- und Ausländerwesens

Aufgaben auf dem III H, I, M, Wi, N und Kgf.-Gebiet

Wehrgeistige Führung

Politisch-weltanschauliche Schulung

Geistige Betreuung

Durchführung der Propaganda entsprechend den über AO gegebenen Weisungen

Vorschlag für Einsatz der Prop.Kp.

*) ...

Document 4: Ic/AO Intelligence Group, Table of Organization.

UNITED NATIONS WAR CRIMES COMMISSION

_____YUGOSLAV_____ CHARGES AGAINST_____GERMAN_____ WAR CRIMINALS

CASE No.___R/N/684_____ *

Name of accused, his rank and unit, or official position: (_Not to be translated._)	Kurt(?) WALDHEIM, Oberleutnant. Abwehroffizer with the Ic - Abteilung des Generalstabes der Heeresgruppe E from April 1944 until the capitulation of Germany. (F.25572)
Date and place of commission of alleged crime.	From April 1944 - May 1945. All parts of Yugoslavia.
Number and description of crime in war crimes list.	II. Putting Hostages to Death. I. Murder.
References to relevant provisions of national law.	Violation of Articles 23 b & c, 46 and 50, of the Hague Regulations, 1907, and Article 3, para. 3 of the Law concerning Crimes against the People and the State, 1945.

SHORT STATEMENT OF FACTS.

Oberleutnant WALDHEIM, the German Abwehroffizier with the Ic. staff of the"Heeresgruppe E", headed by General LOEHR, is responsible for the retaliation actions carried out by the Wehrmacht units in Yugoslavia, inasmuch as the "Heeresgruppe E" was involved in directing the retaliation orders issued by the OKW. Thus the Ic. staff of the "Heeresgruppe E" were the means for the massacre of numerous sections of the Serb population.

TRANSMITTED BY_____YUGOSLAV STATE COMMISSION :

* Insert serial number under which the case is registered in the files of the National Office of the accusing State.
(6188) Wt.P.2124/27 5m. 2/46. C. & Co. 714(8)   13th February, 1948.

Document 5: Pages from Kurt Waldheim's United Nations war crimes file.

PARTICULARS OF EVIDENCE IN SUPPORT

The files concerning this charge are in the possession of the Yugoslav War Crimes Commission.

1. Johann K...R stated the following:" I joined the Heeresgruppe E on 3rd April, 1944 as a personal division clerk. The commander was Liet.Col. Warnstorff and his deputy was Waldheim. He was an Ordnanzofficier. His duties were those of an intelligence officer. It was up to him to bring up suggestions concerning reprisal actions, treatment of prisoners of war and civilian internees. . . I remember certain persons having been murdered at Sarajevo in November, 1944. They were executed according to the order given by Waldheim in retalliation for murderxxxof desertion from the German army of some other persons. . . ."

2. Klaus MELINGCHOFF stated that measures of reprisal and retaliation were applied by the German general staff and high-ranking German officers. The same line of action was taken by the accused.

Document Abt.Ia/F No 296/40 Geh. Issued by"Oberfehlshaber Suedost" (Oberkommando der Heeresgruppe F. who headed the Heeresgruppe E. and its staff. Extracts of this document are given below :

"Measures of Retaliation:

A. Cases when they are to be applied :

   1. For persons safety. a) in case of assaulting the life or body of a Reich- or Volksdeutscher German citizen; b) a member of allied troops; c) of a person in service with the military occupation authorities, no matter what their nationality; d) Leading officials or members of the Regional Government.

   2. a) If circumstances do not permit identification of individual offenders; b) if the attack was carried out on defenceless persons on political grounds; c) if the attack resulted in injuring or killing, the crime of killing to be assumed in the case of the person not returning after a certain period.

E. Victims to be executed by way of reprisal:

   . . . .

   2. If collaborators and those taking part cannot be found, those who are casually connected, or particularly sympathisers of Communism, are to be executed.

   . . . .

C. All orders which contradict the aforesaid are to be considered as cancelled.

F. The SS., the höheren Polizeiführers (SD) and "Abwehrkommando" organisations are to participate in the selection of those to be detained, as well as hostages, for the purpose of retaliation.

FEDERATIVNA NARODNA REPUBLIKA JUGOSLAVIJA
DRŽAVNA KOMISIJA
ZA UTVRĐIVANJE ZLOČINA
OKUPATORA I NJIHOVIH POMAGAČA

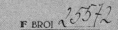
F BROJ 25572

ODLUKA
o utvrđivanju zločina okupatora i njihovih pomagača

ZLOČINAC:

Prezime i ime: _W A L D H E I M (KURT?)_

Približna starost: _____

Narodnost: _____Austrijanac_____

Jedinica, zvanični položaj i čin: _Obe.leutnant, Abwehroffizier na_
službi u Ic—Abteilung des Generalstabes der Heeresgruppe E, u aprilu
1944 do kapitulacije Nemačke.

Poslednje boravište: _____

Ostali lični podaci: _sada u bekstvu_

ŽRTVE ZLOČINA (OŠTEĆENICI):
(sa ličnim podacima)

KRATAK OPIS I KVALIFIKACIJA ZLOČINA:

Ubistva i pokolji.= Streljanja talaca.= Namerno rušenje i pusto=
šenje imovine.= paležem naselja i sl.= (čl.3 tač. 3 jugoslovenskog
Zakona o krivičnim delima protiv naroda i države u vezi sa odredbama
čl.23 b), c), i g), 46 i 50 Haškog Reglmana od 1907 god., i sa od=
redbama čl. II tač. 1 b) Zakona br. X Kontrolnog Saveta za Nemačku
od 20.12.1945 god.)

Document 6: First page of the Yugoslav file against Kurt Waldheim.

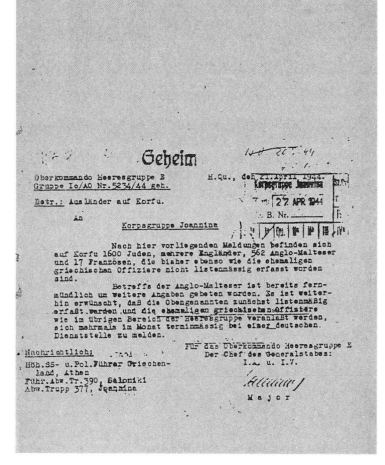

Geheim

Oberkommando Heeresgruppe E   H.Qu., den 21.April 1944.
Gruppe Ic/AO Nr.5234/44 geh.

Betr.: Ausländer auf Korfu.   7 = 27. APR 1944

An
                 Korpsgruppe Joannina

          Nach hier vorliegenden Meldungen befinden sich
auf Korfu 1600 Juden, mehrere Engländer, 562 Anglo-Malteser
und 17 Franzosen, die bisher ebenso wie die ehemaligen
griechischen Offiziere nicht listenmässig erfasst worden
sind.
          Betreffs der Anglo-Malteser ist bereits fern-
mündlich um weitere Angaben gebeten worden. Es ist weiter-
hin erwünscht, daß die Obengenannten zunächst listenmäßig
erfaßt werden und die ehemaligen griechischen Offiziere
wie im übrigen Bereich der Heeresgruppe veranlaßt werden,
sich mehrmals im Monat terminmässig bei einer deutschen
Dienststelle zu melden.

                                   Für das Oberkommando Heeresgruppe E
Nachrichtlich: Der Chef des Generalstabes:
                                   I.A. u. I.V.
Höh.SS- u.Pol.Führer Griechen-
     land, Athen
Führ.Abw.Tr.390, Saloniki
Abw.Trupp 377, Jeannina   *Hammer*/
                                                Major

Document 7: Communication sent by Major Hammer, deputy chief of the Ic/AO group, ordering the registration of Jews and foreigners on the island of Corfu.

9-22-1943   Army Group South Greece,
21,30 h   Dept. Ia
                        (stamped) SECRET
                                (stamped) DRAFT

Secret!

Long distance telephone call from First Lieutnant Frey to First
Lieutnant Waldheim

1. Italians on the Peloponnes concentrated in reception camps Tripoly-
   Megalopoly-Kalamata.
   From there transport by rail to Athens. In Athens arrived to date:
       1,308 (?) officers and 23,749 NCO's and ratings.
   Remaining in the above named reception camps:
       7,318 officers, NCO's and ratings.
   Under way to Athens at this time:
       2,400 officers, NCO's and ratings.
   Withhold approximately 2,000 rank and file as workers. Total
   evacuation to be completed within 3 to 4 days.
2. Evacuation of Italians from Attika and Böothia completed except for
   smaller handling units. 4,598 rank and file remain in Athens for labor
   employment.

                   Army Group South Greece
                   Dept Ia-o 1, No. 1280 (?) 43 secr.
                           9-22-1943
                 (initialled "W")

Document 8: Translation of Waldheim's telephone report referring to
the transportation of Italian prisoners of war. (Transcript.)

	Box numbers	Thickness of file (ins.)
Belgium *vs* Germans	14–18	24
Canada *vs* Germans	19	1
China *vs* Germans	19	1/8
Czechoslovakia *vs* Germans	20–22	12
Czechoslovakia *vs* Hungarians	23	1/4
Denmark *vs* Germans	23	4
Ethiopia *vs* Italians	23	1
France *vs* Germans	24–52	121
France *vs* Italians	52	1
Greece *vs* Albanians	53	1/8
Greece *vs* Bulgarians	53–54	8
Greece *vs* Germans	55–56	8
Greece *vs* Italians	57	4
Luxembourg *vs* Germans	58–59	8
The Netherlands *vs* Germans	60–68	36
Norway *vs* Germans	69	5
Poland *vs* Germans	70–89	96
United Kingdom *vs* Germans	90–103	66
United Kingdom *vs* Italians	103–104	6
United Kingdom *vs* Rumanians	104	1/8
USA *vs* Italians	105	6
USA *vs* Germans	105–108	18
Yugoslavia *vs* Albanians	109	1/8
Yugoslavia *vs* Bulgarians	109	4
Yugoslavia *vs* Germans	110–116	36
Yugoslavia *vs* Hungarians	117	1/2
Yugoslavia *vs* Italians	117–119	12
Australia *vs* Japanese	120	2
France *vs* Japanese	120	1/4
United Kingdom *vs* Japanese	120	2
USA *vs* Japanese	121–123	12
WCC charges	124	1

Adjourned cases: Czechoslovakia, Denmark, Belgium, France, Greece, Luxembourg, The Netherlands, Poland, United Kingdom, USA, Yugoslavia, Australia. *Box nos.* 125–130, 30 ins.

Colonel Hodgson's file: Miscellaneous drafts, 1944–5, notes, Committee I meetings 1945, miscellaneous papers *re* Yugoslav charges and United Kingdom charges, Nos. 1087 and 1365. *Box no.* 131, 5 ins.

Committee I, Notes on Cases, August 1945–March 1948, typed, unbound.
Box no. 131, 1 ins.

Correspondence with National Offices *re* charges, arranged by country, Australia–Yugoslavia. *Box nos.* 132–133, 8 ins.

Registers of Charge Files, showing registration and numbering of Charge Files, chronologically arranged, 7 bound volumes. *Box nos.* 134–135, 12 ins.

Document 10: Breakdown of the recently declassified portion of the UN war crimes files. (Transcript.)

Personenstandesblatt

für die Meldung von Beamten und Angestellten bei m.

Bezirksgericht Baden bei Wien

Raum für Lichtbild

Zuname:	-Dr. WALDHEIM
Vorname:	Kurt
Titel:	...ssor (K)

Militärdienst: Von — bis:	15.August 1939 bis 9.Mai 1945
Feldzüge:	Frankreich, Russland, Balkan
Verwundungen:	Gr.Splitter r.Unterschenkel

Wehrverbände der NSDAP (SS, SA, NSKK, NSFK), Eintrittstag, Zeitraum der Dauer:	NS-Reiterkorps.
Letzte Dienststelle:	
Funktionen:	keine.

Document ii: Cuttings from Kurt Waldheim's *curriculum vitae*, 5 November 1945.

Beograd, 12.decembar 1947 g.

3939/47

Pr.Pov.Br. 3939/47

MINISTARSTVU INOSTRANIH POSLOVA
=Odeljenju za medjunarodne organizacije=

B E O G R A D

Od strane Ministarstva unutrašnjih poslova FNRJ-odeljenja
za ratne zarobljenike-aktom Pov.br.4725 od 17.IX.1947 g. dostavljen
nam je materijal istrage o izvesnim nemačkim zarobljenicima i dr.,
pripadnicima štaba biv. nemačke "Heeresgruppe E", kojom je koman=
dovao osuđeni ratni zločinac, general Lochr, posebno o pripadnicima
Abwehra i tzv. odeljenja Ic) u okviru toga štaba. Izmedju ostalih
najvažnijih pripadnika ovih ustanova, čije se vođstvo nalazi u
Nemačkoj, kao i u Austriji, a za koje postoje podaci o zločinaškoj
aktivnosti u našoj zemlji za vreme okupacije, nalazi se i poručnik
Waldheim, za koga jedan svedok-nemački zarobljenik potvrđuje da
je radio na određivanju mera odmazde putem streljanja talaca
(laufeuden Geiselaugelegeuheiteu). O tome licu saopšteni su nam pome=
nutim aktom sledeći podaci:

"Poručnik Waldheim,jedan stari,već ilegalni nacionalsocijalis=
ta, koji je u zapisniku naveden kao nadležan za taoce i
koji je održavao vezu sa V- ljudima (poverljivim ljudima),
se danas nalazi u Austriji ne samo kao slobodan,već je zapo=
slen kao sekretar u inostranom uredu (Legationssekretaer)
in Auswaertigen Amt). On pripada pratnji austriskog minis=
tra spoljnih poslova Dr.Grubera i bio je sa njim u Londo=
nu. Ova stvar i za ovdašnje ministarstvo inostranih poslova
sigurno nije od manje vrednosti."

Dostavljamo vam ove podatke radi eventualne upotrebe, s
obzirom na aktivnost austriskog ministra spoljnih poslova Dr.Grubera
protivu naših nacionalnih interesa. Izvestite nas, da li je potrebno
s tim u vezi sačiniti odluku za Gruberovog saradnika poručnika
Waldheima, na osnovu koje bi bio registrovan kod Komisije Ujedinje=
nih Naroda za ratne zločine (imati u vidu da krajni rok za registra=
ciju ističe završetkom godine).

SMRT FAŠIZMU — SLOBODA NARODU

Po o./PRETSEDNIKA
NAČELNIK PRAVNOG ODELJENJA,

(Uroš M. Bjelić)

M./A.

3937

Izv.pov.br.3939/47

Beograd, 26 decembar 1947.

MINISTARSTVU INOSTRANIH POSLOVA
- Odeljenje za medjunarodne organizacije -

Predmet: WALDHEIM
dostava odluke.

B E O G R A D

U vezi našeg dopisa broj gornji od 12 t.m. u prilogu dostav=
ljamo vam našu odluku F.br.25572 od 18.XII.1947 god. kojom je utvrđen
i proglašen za ratnog zločinca bivši Oberleutnant, Abwehroffizier na
službi Ic-Apteilung des Generalstabes der Heeresgrupe E, WALDHEIM, po
imenu verovatno Kurt, za koga smo vam već javili da sada pripada prat=
nji austriskog Ministra Dr. Grubera.

Mi smo pod gornjim brojem danas dostavili tome Ministarstvu -
II regionalno odeljenje - dopis s molbom da dostavi našu prijavu Komi=
siji ujedinjenih naroda za ratne zločine u Londonu radi njegovog regi=
strovanja i stavljanja na listu nemačkih ratnih zločinaca, istučći
našu osobitu važnost za njegovim registrovanjem.

SMRT FAŠIZMU — SLOBODA NARODU!

Pretsednik
Državne komisije

Exp. 29-XII-47   b kuj. 30.XI.47

/Dr. Dušan Neljković/

Bo5/Pe

(Name und Adresse der anfragenden Dienststelle)

United States Mission
Berlin Document Center
Wasserkäfersteig 1
1000 Berlin 37

Datum: Tel. 20.3.1979 Sch

2004798

Es wird um Feststellung gebeten, ob im Berlin Document Center Unterlagen über folgende Person vorliegen:

Vor- und Zuname:	Kurt W a l d h e i m
Geburtsort:	n.F.
Geburtsdatum:	21.12.1918
Beruf:	
Gegenwärtige Adresse:	
Auskünfte werden erbeten über:	

Zur Ermittlung von Unterlagen in den Archiven des Berlin Document Center ist die genaue Angabe des Vor- und Zunamens sowie des Geburtsdatums unbedingt erforderlich. In Ausnahmefällen, in denen die genauen Personalien nicht bekannt sind, sind Einzelheiten über evtl. Dienststellung, Dienstgrad, Einsatzorte bzw. Heimatstandorte sowie Einsatzzeitpunkte usw. anzugeben. (Angaben, wie Herbert Schulze, Krim.Ang., genügen nicht!)

In der Rubrik „Auskünfte werden erbeten über" ist zu vermerken, an welchen Informationen die anfragende Dienststelle im einzelnen interessiert ist, z. B.: Mitgliedschaften in Parteien und politischen Organisationen, Zugehörigkeit zur Wehrmacht, Waffen-SS, Schupo, Kripo, Gestapo, Organisation Todt, Arbeitsdienst usw., Einzelheiten über den beruflichen Werdegang (einschließlich Eintrittsdaten, Dienstgrade und Dienststellungen, Beförderungs- und Versetzungsdaten, Einheiten und Dienststellen), Verwundungen, Erkrankungen, Lazarettaufenthalte, Auszeichnungen, Staatsangehörigkeit, Vorstrafen, Inhaftierungen, Verurteilungen usw. Die Erteilung einer Generalauskunft über die angefragte Person erfolgt nur in besonderen Fällen, wenn ausdrücklich darum gebeten wird.

Telefon-Nr.	Unterschrift

(Diese Rubriken werden vom Berlin Document Center ausgefüllt)

	Pos.	Neg.			Pos.	Neg.			Pos.	Neg.
1. NSDAP-Zentralkartei			7. SA			✓	13. NS-Lehrerbund			
2. Anträge		✓	8. OPG			✓	14. Reichsärztekammer			
3. PK		✓	9. RWA			✓	15. Parteist. Erhebung			
4. SS-Führer			10. EWZ			✓	16. NS-Frauenschaft			
5. RuSHA		✓	11. Kulturkammer			✓	17.			
6. Versch. SS-Unterlagen			12. Volksgerichtshof			✓	18.			

(Erklärungen zu den Abkürzungen finden Sie auf der Rückseite)

BERLIN DOCUMENT CENTER
Keine Unterlagen vorhanden

Eingangsdatum	Ausgangsdatum
	MAR 22 1979

Document 13: Berlin Document Centre Report, indicating Waldheim's non-membership of any Nazi organizations.

Document 12a and b: December 1947 correspondence between the Yugoslav Ministry of Interior and the Belgrade Foreign Ministry concerning Kurt Waldheim.

SPISAK STRANACA

čiji je dolazak u FNRJ nepoželjan

(Završen 20.XI 1952.)

30.293   I primerak

HAMMER ,potpukovnik nemačke vojske,u gradjanstvu direktor
banke u EMSU,redjen 1892.ili 1897.Od leta 1942.de
decembra 1944.rukovodilac u I/c odelenju AO(Abver
ofecir)Armijske grupe "E".

...

WALDHEIM,poručnik nemačke vojske,redjen 1918.Do polevine
1942.na službi u Štabu za vezu kod italijanske
armijske grupe 9 i 11 u Atini,a zatim u Komandi
12.AOK.Od 1945.premešten u Istru.

...

WARNSTORFF,nemački generalštabni potpukovnik,redjen 1908.
U 1944 bio I c oficir nemačke Armijske grupe "E"
u Solunu i u Sarajevu.

...

Izostavljeno 30.290 drugih imena čiji je dolazak u FNRJ
nepoželjan

Document 14: A 1952 Yugoslav document, listing Waldheim as a war criminal, which may have been used to intimidate him.

own citizens.'[1] But true to Austrian tradition the legation in
Prague issued 5,000 visas a day. A total of 93,000 Czechs
received asylum in Austria. The WJC have implied that in
sending his instructions to the Austrian legation in Prague,
Foreign Minister Waldheim was responding to pressure from
the Soviets. This appears unlikely.

Waldheim has pointed out that the cable was issued by the
Ministry of Interior, which was really responsible for the
matter. As Foreign Minister he merely initialled the document since it reflected the policy of the Vienna cabinet. A
spokesman for the Austrian government said the directive was
'issued for security reasons because thousands of visa applications had been stolen from the facility in Prague'.[2] But this
does not tell the whole story.

During the crisis there was great apprehension among
Austrians over a possible move by the Soviets against their
small neutral country. As Waldheim wrote in his memoirs:
'The Austrian government had to tread something of a tight-
rope'.[3] This is confirmed by a scholar who notes that during
the invasion of Czechoslovakia, the Austrian cabinet 'saw the
need for prudence to avoid unduly twisting the tail of the
Russian bear'.[4]

According to Waldheim, 'Russian planes violated our
skies', making the Austrians apprehensive of a move against
their country. Waldheim later found that these fears were not
unfounded since the Soviets 'received wrong reports that
NATO forces had entered Austrian territory from Bavaria
clandestinely in order to build up a position along the Austro-
Czech border'.[5] Clearly Waldheim's consent to the 21 August

1. *Chicago Tribune*, 31 October 1986.
2. *Chicago Tribune*, 1 November 1986.
3. Waldheim, *In the Eye of the Storm*, p. 31.
4. Thomas O. Schlesinger, *Austrian Neutrality in Pre-War Europe*, p. 54.
5. Waldheim, *In the Eye of the Storm*, p. 32.

cable ordering the closing of the Prague embassy was motivated by genuine concern over the possible Soviet reaction rather than any blackmail based on his UNWCC file.

In 1970 Waldheim returned to the UN where two years later he was elected Secretary General. An examination of his tenure as UN chief reveals that as with other stages of his career much that has been written is contradicted by the evidence.

CHAPTER V

The Spokesman of Humanity

An important part of the Waldheim mythology, which is accepted by many of the people who support the case against him, is the belief that he was an agent of the Soviets and an enemy of Israel while he served as Secretary General. This legend has surprisingly wide acceptance despite a total lack of evidence that Waldheim worked against Western interests. Rather, Waldheim's conduct as Secretary General suggests that he made an effort to placate all factions, especially those which had access to his bogus war crimes file.

The former UN Under-Secretary General, the defector Arkady Shevchenko, notes that 'Waldheim tried to retain the favour of all sides – this was his main weakness'.[1] Another Under Secretary General, Brian Urquhart, recalls Waldheim's 'innate dislike for coming down firmly on one side or the other'.[2] Urquhart notes that on one occasion the Secretary General could not decide on the wording of a statement on Vietnam so that he told Waldheim, 'We really must make a decision.'

'There will be no decision,' he snapped back. 'That is a decision.' Another UN Secretariat member observed that, to avoid giving offence, Waldheim 'equivocated endlessly on every minute decision with aides long into the night'. This same official states, 'Waldheim was particularly vulnerable to lobbying from missions that wanted to get their nationals in high positions.'[3]

Waldheim was especially careful to avoid offending

1. Arkady Shevchenko, *Breaking With Moscow*, p. 393.
2. Brian Urquhart, *A Life in Peace and War*, p. 229.
3. *New York Times*, 16 June 1986.

representatives of the superpowers. Indeed, his memoirs make it clear that he believed a Secretary General cannot function without the complete support of the USA and USSR. This was resented by the delegates of the Third World countries who criticized Waldheim while he was in office because he 'accommodates too readily to superpower demands'.[1] More recently many experts have concluded that 'both the Soviet Union and United States must have known that Mr Waldheim had concealed his past because as Secretary General he responded to pressure from the superpowers'.[2] On a wide range of issues including Iran, Afghanistan and South East Asia, Waldheim showed a marked willingness to serve the interests of the Soviet Union and the United States. He often reduced himself to the level of an errand boy for the superpowers.

Waldheim came to office during the era of *détente* in 1971 by which time the Americans and Russians were exasperated with the UN because of the actions of the previous Secretaries General. Dag Hammarskjöld had clashed with the Russians over Africa and the Middle East. Soviet leader Nikita Khrushchev (who banged his shoe on the table at the UN in protest in 1960) said of Hammarskjöld, 'We must get rid of him.' It has been suggested that the KGB was responsible for Hammarskjöld's mysterious death.[3] Secretary General U Thant had identified with the Third World and clashed with the Americans especially over Vietnam. By 1971 both superpowers were determined that there would not be another Secretary General who opposed their policies. Waldheim was the ideal candidate for Secretary General since both sides had information that could force his resignation if he dared to cross their interests. In 1971 Waldheim

1. *New York Times* (Magazine), 13 September 1981.
2. *New York Times*, 14 June 1986.
3. Shevchenko, *Breaking with Moscow*, p. 134.

himself stated 'the antecedents of each candidate' for the office of Secretary General are 'scrutinized carefully by members of the Security Council'.[1] More recently, on 2 April 1986, Waldheim told UPI that in 1971 it had been 'established that I am clear' because of an investigation of him by the CIA and KGB. As we shall see, a former high-ranking CIA official has recently suggested that the agency knew of Waldheim's hidden past when he was being considered for Secretary General. Perhaps the CIA saw Waldheim's file as insurance for good behaviour.

When the time arrived to elect a Secretary General in autumn 1971, Waldheim indicates that with regard to his candidacy, 'the Western powers could be described as generally friendly but non-committal',[2] with the Soviets expressing similar sentiments. The problem for Waldheim was the Chinese. It may of course be more than a coincidence that they were the only permanent members of the Security Council who did not have access to his hidden files. The Chinese vetoed Waldheim twice but on the third ballot they abstained, thus permitting his election.

According to contemporary reports the Soviets were delighted with Waldheim's election. 'He was their real choice from the beginning,' commented a British diplomat 'because they figured he wouldn't be an activist Secretary General.' Another observer noted that Waldheim was 'entirely acceptable to Washington'.[3] Waldheim himself commented: 'Those who know me better know that I am a very active man but one has to know the limits of activities within the framework of a mandate.' Everyone understood that Waldheim was not the type of man to launch independent initiatives that would embarrass his superpower patrons. In his memoirs

1. Kurt Waldheim, *The Austrian Example*, p. 9.
2. Waldheim, *In the Eye of the Storm*, p. 36.
3. *Time* magazine, 3 January 1972; *Newsweek*, 3 January 1972.

Waldheim claims that in 1971 he had become 'the conscience of mankind' and 'the spokesman of humanity'. But as Secretary General he would serve other interests.

Waldheim was a strong supporter of US Secretary of State Henry Kissinger's policy of *détente* between the superpowers. During the 1970s, while tensions between the Soviet Union and the United States persisted, there were frequent examples of co-operation. According to Shevchenko, the Soviet Foreign Minister Andrei Gromyko 'believed the United States to be not only the Soviet Union's adversary but also its partner as the interests of both nations – whether temporary or long term – are parallel or coincide'.[1] At the United Nations during the 1970s the interests of the superpowers frequently coincided. Indeed Waldheim's entire approach was based on the assumption that the Cold War was over in the world organization. He wrote, 'East–West rivalries while still predominant in global terms have become relatively less predominant in United Nations affairs.'[2]

The 1970s saw the rising tide of the Third World countries in the UN. During this period the neutral countries of Africa, Asia and Latin America became a considerable majority in the General Assembly. It was believed that future Secretaries General would come from the Third World. Waldheim was regarded as 'the last Secretary General who is committed to Western democracy'.[3] The superpowers preferred a man like Waldheim who had ties to both the Soviets and the Western bloc rather than someone from the Third World who distrusted the Russians and Americans.

1. Shevchenko, *Breaking with Moscow*, p. 199.
2. Waldheim, *In the Eye of the Storm*, p. 112. One scholar noted that in the 1970s 'the UN's concerns have shifted from East–West to a North–South axis': John Stoessinger, *The United Nations and the Superpowers*, p. 213.
3. *New York Times* Magazine, 13 September 1981.

Waldheim supported the Nixon administration's policy of *détente* despite Kissinger's low opinion of him. In his memoirs Kissinger notes how he used the subservient Secretary General. 'One could be sure that he would convey what one was reluctant to say directly – veiled threats or plans for compromise too delicate to put forward under one's own name.'[1] Waldheim certainly acted as if the Americans had some type of control over him.

In policy matters Waldheim tried to accommodate the Americans. Thus, for example, he expressed a willingness to help speed up the opening of a North Vietnamese observer mission at the United Nations but he dropped the planned initiative after Kissinger objected. On a wide range of other issues Waldheim accommodated the USA.

The Iranian hostage crisis was an example of Waldheim's willingness to serve American interests. On 10 November 1979, a few days after the embassy in Tehran was seized, American Secretary of State Cyrus Vance came to New York to work out with Waldheim a package of proposals that the USA would offer to the Khomeini government in exchange for the release of the hostages. The Americans promised to allow the Iranians to initiate legal claims in the US courts in order to obtain the Shah's assets removed illegally from Iran. The Americans also pledged to support an international commission to inquire into human rights violations in Iran under the Shah's regime if Khomeini would release the embassy personnel.

Several weeks later the US ambassador to the UN, Donald McHenry, suggested that the Secretary General should go himself to Iran to present the proposals but Waldheim realized that 'the auguries were not good'.[2] Indeed, one

1. Henry Kissinger, *Years of Upheaval*, p. 455.
2. Waldheim, *In the Eye of the Storm*, p. 4.

author notes that Waldheim's usual 'actuarial instinct failed him' during the hostage crisis.[1] His willingness to undertake such a hopeless mission reflects Waldheim's subservience to American interests. Secretary of State Cyrus Vance called Waldheim's planned trip 'a triumph of US diplomacy'.[2] The Iranians saw Waldheim as 'a stooge of the Great Satan scheming to get to know Iran's position so as to better protect the interests of his master, the United States'.[3]

Incredibly, Waldheim went to Tehran even though several Security Council members which had voted for the resolution proposing his mission had withdrawn their support, while the Iranians had made it clear that he was not welcome.

When Waldheim landed in Tehran, the Ayatollah Khomeini commented, 'I do not trust this man'.[4] The Secretary General was in for a rough reception from Iranians who shared the attitude of their theocratic ruler. 'Waldheim was treated to a grotesque meeting with a large group of mutilated and deformed individuals, allegedly victims of SAVAK [Iranian secret police] who screamed and waved stumps of missing limbs in his face.'[5] Waldheim's visit to the cemetery of the martyrs of the revolution turned into a riot that had to be cut short out of concern for his life. 'Do you think we shall ever get out of here alive?' Waldheim asked an aide. He wondered to himself 'whether it was the duty of the UN Secretary General representing the world community to undertake such mission impossibles'.[6]

Waldheim's humiliation in Tehran was only beginning. Ayatollah Khomeini refused to grant an audience to a man he

---

1. Thomas M. Franck, *Nation Against Nation*, p. 141.
2. *New York Times*, 13 December 1979.
3. Waldheim, *In the Eye of the Storm*, p. 6.
4. *New York Times*, 31 December 1977.
5. Gary Sick, *All Fall Down*, p. 278.
6. Waldheim, *In the Eye of the Storm*, p. 9.

considered an American errand boy. Waldheim was also refused a meeting with the hostages. The Secretary General's trip to Tehran may have been in Cyrus Vance's view 'a triumph for American diplomacy', but it was a fiasco for the prestige of Waldheim and the world organization he headed.

The hostage crisis would eventually be resolved in secret talks between the Americans and Iranians in which Waldheim and the UN did not play any significant role. Despite his staunch support of the Carter administration Waldheim was never taken into the confidence of the Americans. Waldheim realized his subordinate role. Thus, he wrote: 'I harbour some resentment at the lack of information about these shadowy negotiations.'[1] This did not stop him from serving American interests on numerous other occasions.

This was particularly true in the Greek–Turkish dispute over Cyprus. According to Brian Urquhart, 'The Greek lobby in Washington is powerful and in 1976, without movement in the Cyprus problem the Congress would not vote for military aid appropriations for Turkey which is an essential member of NATO. Thus the Secretary General's negotiations on the Cyprus problem and their perceived success were and are important for Washington.'[2] It is no wonder that Waldheim writes in his memoirs that the Cyprus issue 'took up more time and attention during my years in office than any other confrontation'.[3]

In July 1974 the Turks invaded Cyprus: this greatly aggravated the long-standing controversy between the Greeks and Turkish communities on the embattled island. In February 1975 the 'Turkish Federated State of Cyprus' was created in the area of the island under control of the Turkish military. Waldheim undertook exhaustive negotiations in an effort to

1. Ibid, p. 161.
2. Urquhart, *A Life in Peace and War*, p. 265.
3. Waldheim, *In the Eye of the Storm*, p. 78.

end the conflict between Turks and Greeks. Urquhart referred to the Cyprus talks as 'the most frustrating negotiations in my experience'.[1] The Cyprus negotiations ran on for years with no agreement ever being reached. The central issue was always the same – Greek demands for a unitary government for the island while the Turkish minority demanded partition. On a number of occasions, Waldheim believed he was close to a negotiated settlement only to find the deal coming apart overnight. Although Waldheim was never able to achieve a settlement, Kissinger praised him for his 'unfailing constructive role', which the pliable Secretary General appreciated.

Waldheim was a man who enjoyed publicity. Indeed, when the Secretary General walked the streets of New York he was 'sorry no one recognized him'.[2] (It is not to his credit that this would no longer be true!) Shevchenko speaks of Waldheim's 'love of grandeur. He likes to be the centre of attention and would accordingly indulge himself in small matters.' Indeed, there is a story circulating at the UN that after Waldheim left as Secretary General he asked the Austrian UN mission to send him American toilet paper.

Waldheim revelled in ceremony. In his memoirs he bemoans that as Secretary General, he was sometimes given the reception of a Foreign Minister instead of being treated as a Prime Minister as suggested in UN protocol. Waldheim is certainly no man of the people. Indeed, he criticized President Carter for jogging in public since it 'did little to enhance his prestige'.[3] Waldheim's pettiness was legendary. He was a man who saw only the trees but never the wood. American ambassador to the UN, Daniel P. Moynihan, noted that Waldheim functioned as a postal clerk who operated along

1. Urquhart, *A Life in Peace and War*, p. 259.
2. *New York Times* (Magazine), 13 September 1981.
3. Waldheim, *In the Eye of the Storm*, p. 169.

'Austro-Hungarian lines'.[1] Kissinger called Waldheim 'a great gossip'.

Under-Secretary General Brian Urquhart probably knew Waldheim as well as anyone, and has drawn a striking portrait of the man in his recent book. Urquhart notes that Waldheim was not devoid of positive characteristics, including great physical stamina, occasional statesmanship and even courage. But what emerges is a man unfit for such a high position since 'he lacked the qualities of vision, integrity, inspiration and leadership that the United Nations desperately needed'.[2] Urquhart regarded Waldheim as 'an energetic ambitious mediocrity'. He bemoans the fact that Waldheim was not an independent internationalist 'in the Hammarskjöld tradition', which would be 'a prospect certainly not welcome to the Soviet Union and possibly not to other great powers either'.

In particular Urquhart notes that the Secretary General was 'too anxious to be given credit and tended to be too accessible to the media'. According to Urquhart: 'This need for constant public recognition deprived Waldheim's office of two qualities which in his lack of real power are essential for the Secretary General – dignity and mystery.' He once told Waldheim, 'if the Loch Ness monster came ashore and gave a press conference it would never be heard from again, but he didn't get the point'.

Urquhart noted that the Secretary General wanted a larger aircraft since he 'clearly wished to emulate Kissinger's practice of taking the press corps with him as a captive audience'. Waldheim 'seemed to believe that a good proposal or performance had no validity unless it was publicly reported'.

In 1976, when his first term of office was running out, Waldheim's tendency to court both the press and the key

---

1. Daniel P. Moynihan, *A Dangerous Place*, p. 83.
2. Urquhart, *A Life in Peace and War*, p. 228.

member governments greatly increased. Waldheim would do anything to remain in office. According to Arkady Shev-chenko, 're-election became an obsession with Waldheim who was willing to pay too high a price for it. The work of the Secretariat slowed to a crawl as the result of the emphasis on re-electioning.'[1] Urquhart notes that in the autumn of 1976 there were

several tiresome weeks of rumours and intrigue which brought out the worst in Waldheim and drove him to woo the press and governments in the most assiduous manner. This was a far cry from the dignity and restraint of Hammarskjöld and U Thant when faced with similar situations, and my doubts about Waldheim surfaced once more. He seemed to be a man without real substance, quality or character, swept along by an insatiable thirst for public office.[2]

To win re-election to a second five-year term as Secretary General, Waldheim had to gain the support or at least the abstention of all five permanent members of the Security Council including the USSR. A spokesman for the Soviet UN mission claimed in 1986 that before the 1971 and 1976 elections 'No attempt was made to investigate Mr Waldheim. The Soviet Union knew nothing.'[3] This is of course impossible since the Soviets as routine procedure investigate every detail about people of a much lower rank than Waldheim. But no investigation may have been necessary when Waldheim became Secretary General since the Soviets probably were aware of the bogus war crimes file that had been prepared against the young diplomat in 1947. As in 1971 the Soviets and Americans voted Waldheim into office in 1976 without any mention of his hidden past.

Though largely ignored by the US news media, Waldheim's relations with the Soviets while he was UN

1. Shevchenko, *Breaking with Moscow*, p. 397.
2. Urquhart, *A Life in Peace and War*, p. 268.
3. *New York Times*, 8 April 1986.

Secretary General certainly make an intriguing story. It is perhaps no coincidence that the two highest Soviet officials to serve at the UN in that period have turned out to be involved with US intelligence. Viktor Lessiovsky, an aide to the Secretary General, who over a period of many years provided considerable intelligence to the FBI, and Arkady Shevchenko who defected to the CIA in 1978 are two of the most important figures in the Waldheim case.

Shevchenko, who now lives in the USA, has claimed in recent interviews that neither the CIA or KGB knew about Waldheim's UNWCC file. It is not surprising that he would say that since he is under CIA protection and he would say nothing to embarrass the agency. The fact that the CIA through Shevchenko has not chosen to claim that the KGB knew about Waldheim suggests that the American intelligence agency is honouring an agreement with the KGB. Shevchenko notes that while he was at the UN, 'KGB expanded its methods of getting people on the hook. This meant blackmailing them to force their co-operation.'[1]

In his book, published before the Waldheim revelations, Shevchenko curiously goes out of his way to deny that the KGB had access to the UNWCC files and to refute the charge that Viktor Lessiovsky gained any information while working for Kurt Waldheim. According to Shevchenko:

... there were only two UN operations in New York where KGB penetration efforts were frustrated. One was the organization's secret archives. Soviet spymasters waged a steady campaign to place their agents in positions which would give them access to the minutes of confidential meetings and to copies of classified cables.[2]

It is certainly incredible that Shevchenko would claim that the KGB could not penetrate the UN archives. From my own

1. Shevchenko, *Breaking with Moscow*, p. 316.
2. Ibid, p. 331.

experiences in 1979, it is clear that there was no security to speak of at the UN archives. It is not possible that the KGB with all its super-sophisticated technology could not penetrate the UN archives in the 1970s. Indeed, one official seriously suggested to me that there were no guards at the UN archives at night because it was expected that various intelligence organizations would penetrate the security no matter how elaborate and it was best to avoid an incident. 'There are no secrets at the UN' is the unspoken rule. Everyone operates under the assumption that in a multinational organization it is pointless to attempt to keep secrets.

Why did Shevchenko claim that the Soviets could not get into the UN archives? It is quite possible that when he wrote his book he anticipated the disclosure some day of Waldheim's UNWCC file and he wished to make it appear unlikely that the KGB or CIA had access to the Secretary General's embarrassing dossier. It is generally assumed that Shevchenko's book was carefully supervised if not written by the CIA. US intelligence may have inserted the passage without explaining its meaning to the Soviet defector.

Shevchenko also makes a point of denying that the KGB agent Viktor Lessiovsky obtained any secrets from Waldheim:

The Secretary General's office, at least under Kurt Waldheim, also succeeded in resisting Moscow's attempts to extract sensitive information. Even though a KGB colonel, Viktor Lessiovsky, was a special assistant to the UN chief from 1961 to 1973 and again from 1976 onward, Waldheim's intimates froze him out of the office's most sensitive activities.[1]

It is ludicrous for Shevchenko to suggest that with a KGB colonel on his staff Waldheim could have prevented Soviet intelligence from gaining access to his private papers and other secrets. What makes the story even more fascinating is

1. Ibid, p. 207.

the evidence that Lessiovsky was a double agent working for the FBI. Waldheim notes that Lessiovsky was 'a very easy-going cultivated man. He had a remarkable range of acquaintances in American business and society. One day he even invited Mrs Kennedy, the widow of the president, to have lunch with him.'[1] Indeed, Lessiovsky is believed to be the Soviet double agent Fedora who supplied a great deal of intelligence to the FBI on a wide range of subjects including the Kennedy assassination, the Pentagon papers and Soviet intelligence penetration of Western governments. There is controversy over whether Lessiovsky was loyal to Moscow or Washington.[2] Of course, Lessiovsky may have been Waldheim's contact with the KGB. Or perhaps Lessiovsky and Waldheim were both in the never-never land between rival intelligence organizations playing off one side against the other.

The main losers as a result of the superpower collusion over Kurt Waldheim were the Third World countries. In fact the growing power of the Afro-Asian bloc in the General Assembly was the principal reason the Americans and Russians decided to elect a man like Waldheim as Secretary General. While he served as chief executive of the UN, Waldheim gave lip service to the causes supported by the Third World but his rhetoric was rarely followed by concrete action.

Indeed, Waldheim tried to halt many of the Third World initiatives in the General Assembly. Although he notes that the recommendations of the Assembly were 'without binding effect', Waldheim believed that they frequently had to be stopped because 'over the course of time they are bound to

1. Waldheim, *In the Eye of the Storm*, p. 141.
2. *Newsweek*, 14 September 1981; Arthur Schlesinger, *Robert Kennedy and His Times*, p. 357.

influence thought and action'.[1] He opposed the Third World effort to improve its economic position *vis-à-vis* the developed nations. The Secretary General noted 'the demands of the Third World countries made on the industrialized states offered no comparable rewards. Their more radical leaders seldom based their claims in the context of mutual benefits.' Waldheim had no sympathy for this approach since he never recognized the moral right of the Third World to receive justice from the industrialized states that exploited its resources.

In April 1974 the General Assembly held a special session 'with a view to establish a new system of relations based on equality and the common interest of all states'. According to a spokesman for the Third World, the real issue was 'economic domination of the poor by the rich'. Waldheim firmly opposed the objectives of the special session and its 'Declaration of Programme of Action on the Establishment of New Economic Order'. According to the Secretary General, 'the special session in 1974 was not guided by counsels of moderation'.[2]

Waldheim also declined to support the Third World effort to gain more influence in the World Bank, the International Monetary Fund and the General Agreement on Tariffs and Trade (GATT). The Secretary General wrote: 'All the exhortations contained in the General Assembly resolutions only compounded the frustrations of the developing countries and the irritation of the developed.'

Waldheim was particularly anxious to stop any Third World initiatives directed against Zionism or apartheid. He notes, 'each year we had the same acrimonious debate on issues such as the Middle East and South Africa and similar

1. Waldheim, *In the Eye of the Storm*, p. 112.
2. Ibid, p. 115.

problems'.[1] The Secretary General did his best to keep such Third-World-orientated issues off the General Assembly debate calendar. To him it was '*auf Granit beissen*' (like biting stone) trying to dissuade the Third World countries from pursuing their agenda against imperialism and neo-colonialism. Waldheim was especially diligent in his effort to oppose the Third World's anti-Zionist policy.

To many it is inconceivable that Israel could have been a party to the possible blackmailing of Kurt Waldheim. Most supporters of the Jewish state believe that if the Israelis had known about Waldheim's concealed past they would have immediately denounced him. The press has accepted without comment the Israeli claim that they did not have a copy of the UNWCC list. Besides, Zionists argue that Israel could not have been blackmailing Waldheim since he is usually por-trayed as a bitter critic of the Jewish state.

But according to Brian Urquhart, Waldheim's 'behaviour in the Middle East was no different from what anyone else's would have been.'[2] In recent interviews Waldheim has told Jews that he favoured Israel and Arabs that he supported their side while he served as Secretary General. In reality he was probably as pro-Israeli as he could have been in view of the huge pro-Palestinian majority in the General Assembly. As with the superpowers, Waldheim did nothing to cross the interests of the Israelis, possibly as a result of their possession of his bogus UNWCC file and other embarrassing informa-tion. Of course his decisions were influenced by factors other than his fear that this file would be exposed.

After the attack on Israeli athletes at the 1972 Olympics, Waldheim tried to put the question of terrorism on the agenda of the General Assembly, despite the objections of

1. Ibid, p. 207.
2. *New York Times*, 14 June 1986.

Arab delegates who argued that the real problem was the unresolved Palestinian–Zionist conflict. Waldheim urged the Assembly to move on the terrorism issue since it was becoming 'extraordinarily serious' and that 'it is our duty to act'.[1] The Secretary General argued that 'under the charter of the United Nations a people has the right to use force: not terrorism of course to get independence'. Finally, Waldheim did secure a discussion on terrorism in the Assembly but he was disappointed that no tough measures were passed.

In December 1972 Waldheim met Arafat in Damascus. The Secretary General tried to persuade the Palestinian leader to concede a key Zionist demand. Waldheim recalled: 'I pressed him as to why he could not accept the existence of the state of Israel. If he could not recognize it, I asked why he could not make at least a preliminary gesture in that direction.'[2] But despite Waldheim's continuing efforts Arafat would not relinquish his claim to his homeland.

In 1973, on the eve of the October War, Waldheim visited Israel. Many Jews resented the fact that he refused to wear a *Yarmulka* at Yad Vashem memorial. But this was just another of Waldheim's numerous gaffes. Indeed, at a dinner party at Foreign Minister Abba Eban's home, Brian Urquhart was dismayed to hear Waldheim utter in response to a toast, 'I am very happy to be in your beautiful capital.'[3] Eban told the press that Waldheim's remark represented an official recognition of Jerusalem as the capital of Israel. To correct the error, Urquhart found it necessary to issue a statement of denial signed by Waldheim.

The Secretary General was more careful about detail in 1974 when Arafat visited the UN. The Algerian president of the General Assembly, Abdel Aziz Bouteflika, tried to give

1. Kurt Waldheim, *Challenge of Peace*, p. 45.
2. Waldheim, *In the Eye of the Storm*, p. 194.
3. Urquhart, *A Life in Peace and War*, p. 236.

Arafat head-of-state status by ordering the special chair for heads of state. But this had not been approved by the Secretary General. 'By the time Waldheim discovered the move, it was too late to remove the chair without gravely insulting Bouteflika – nor was it acceptable for Arafat to enjoy the status which the chair symbolized.'[1] Waldheim negotiated a compromise whereby Arafat did not sit in the chair but merely stood by it.

Despite objections from Kurt Waldheim, the UN General Assembly passed a series of pro-Palestinian resolutions. In 1974 it recognized the PLO as the 'representative of the Palestinian people and invited it to participate in its deliberations'. Subsequent resolutions asked the Secretary General to aid the General Assembly's Committee on the Inalienable Rights of the Palestinian People, to enable the Palestinians to establish their right to independence and sovereignty. The General Assembly voted to create within the Secretariat a special unit on Palestinian rights to prepare pro-PLO publications and give them 'maximum publicity through all appropriate means'. Since 1986 Waldheim has been blamed for these resolutions despite the fact that no evidence has been produced to suggest that he supported the General Assembly's pro-Palestinian initiatives.

Certainly the most common distortion is the claim that Waldheim supported the 1975 General Assembly resolution which declared Zionism as a form of racism. But Waldheim makes it clear that he opposed the resolution because it 'did serious damage to the image of the United Nations'.[2] He indicated that he 'did not fail to express to the authors of the resolution and other governments my deep concern at this unfortunate initiative, asking them to avoid similar actions

1. Ibid, p. 261.
2. Waldheim, *In the Eye of the Storm*, p. 44; see also Waldheim's denunciation of the 1975 resolution in *Foreign Affairs* (Fall 1984), p. 104.

which could only harm the prestige of the world organization. At any rate such action was not repeated during my term of office.' Recently Waldheim told a Jewish journalist that he 'would support a campaign to rescind the 1975 resolution'. adding 'I am certainly ready to use my good offices'.[1]

As Secretary General, Waldheim also opposed the effort to exclude Israel from various UN organs. He wrote: 'Whenever possible I have spoken out against such an approach. Not only do such manoeuvres skirt the bounds of legality but they also put at risk the very existence of the world organization, since they bear the seeds of rift and dissent.'[2]

Of course, on occasion Waldheim found it necessary to rebuke Israel. The Secretary General called the rescue of the hostages at Entebbe Airport in Uganda in 1976 'a serious violation of the national sovereignty of a United Nations member state'. But when the Israelis complained, the Secretary General issued three 'clarifications' of his Entebbe statement.

The Secretary General's greatest clash with Israel came in 1978 over its first invasion of Lebanon. According to Waldheim: 'The events of the war seriously strained the relations between Israel and the UN and me personally.'[3] The Lebanon invasion was bound to cause friction between Israel and whoever was Secretary General just as the 1982 Israeli invasion of Lebanon would cause a worldwide outcry.

As revealed in the diaries of Israeli Prime Minister Moshe Sharett, as early as 1954 Moshe Dayan favoured the creation of a puppet Christian state in Lebanon under 'even just a major'.[4] In 1978 Israel found Major Saad Haddad, a leader of the Christian enclave in southern Lebanon. On 13 June

1. *Jewish Week*, 28 August 1987.
2. Waldheim, *In the Eye of the Storm*, p. 263.
3. Ibid, p. 186.
4. Livia Rokach, *Israel's Sacred Terrorism*, p. 29.

Israeli Defence Minister Moshe Dayan announced that his forces were leaving southern Lebanon but they would not turn the evacuated territory over to the UN peacekeepers but instead to their puppet Major Saad Haddad. Waldheim notes: 'I told Ambassador Blum in vigorous language we knew Israel was supporting Haddad and that it was putting us in an impossible position. I told him this sort of activity simply had to stop.'[1] From this point relations between Waldheim and Israel became cooler. But the Secretary General had to make his protest since Israel was endangering the members of the peacekeeping force.

Waldheim's last involvement with Israel came in June 1981 when the Israeli Air Force raided an Iraqi nuclear reactor which it was claimed could be used to manufacture an atom bomb. There was a desire at the UN for a resolution which would include an arms embargo against Israel. Waldheim arranged a meeting at his office between Ambassadors Jeanne Kirkpatrick of the USA and Sa'adoum Hammadi of Iraq. With the assistance of the Secretary General they arranged a meaningless resolution which disapproved of the Israeli raid but provided no sanctions against the unprovoked attack.[2] Predictably the Israelis denounced Ambassador Kirkpatrick, a devoted supporter of the Zionist state, who had worked with Waldheim to prevent a resolution that would have been painful to Israel.

Although he certainly was not subservient to Israel, Waldheim was careful not to oppose any initiative of importance to it. It should be noted that it was the World Jewish Congress and not Israel that initiated the campaign against Waldheim in March 1986. In fact, Israel has never approved

---

1. Waldheim, *In the Eye of the Storm*, p. 197.
2. Urquhart, *A Life in Peace and War*, pp. 328–9; Waldheim, *In the Eye of the Storm*, p. 207; *New York Times* (Magazine), 13 September 1981.

of the decision to expose the former Secretary General's bogus UNWCC file.

This is reflected in the article, 'The Waldheim affair – how the World Jewish Congress blew it', by Shlomo Aveneri, a scholar and former Director General of Israel's Ministry of Foreign Affairs, who frequently represents the viewpoint of the Jewish state.[1] Aveneri makes it clear that the Israeli government is not happy that the WJC have chosen to make public Waldheim's service in Army Group E. He reveals: 'Israel found itself drawn into a major international crisis without preparation and with great constraints placed on its ability to conduct diplomacy according to its own judgement.' Aveneri believes the WJC should not have acted alone because Israel was 'gravely affected by the WJC's activities but ... was [not] adequately consulted before the organization unilaterally decided to make public disclosures'.

The Israeli spokesman was critical of the way the WJC handled the affair. 'The language of some of the WJC spokesmen was at times intemperate and unnecessarily confrontational ... [thus] they sometimes gave the impression not of presenting evidence but of haranguing a jury and passing judgment at the same time.' Aveneri believed that 'because the WJC appeared to be vindictive, ill-prepared and headline seeking, much of the evidence that eventually did emerge was compromised and sometimes lacking in credibility'. In particular Aveneri criticized the WJC's report of 2 June 1986, *Kurt Waldheim's Hidden Past: An Interim Report*, which was the basis of so many newspaper and magazine articles. He correctly notes that no effort was made to put the documents cited in proper perspective. The real meaning of Waldheim's membership of the SA riding club, the Croatian

---

1. *Present Tense*, April–May 1987. For the WJC's scepticism about Israel's denial of having previous knowledge about Waldheim, see page 150n.

medal, and the political attitude of Waldheim's family were not fairly explained. It is ironic that an Israeli government spokesman criticized the validity of the WJC material which has been accepted as valid by the *New York Times* and other American publications.

However, the *New York Times* is closer to the truth when it noted in June 1987, 'the belief now among many diplomats is that Marshal Tito knew about Waldheim all along but found it more useful to keep the knowledge secret'. Tito was close to Waldheim. The former Secretary General writes in his memoirs: 'We used to meet in New York and Belgrade and I was frequently a guest of his on his two-island complex of Brioni in the Adriatic off the Yugoslav coast.'[1] There is considerable evidence that Tito had personal knowledge of the bogus war crimes file prepared by his government against Waldheim in 1947. An aide of the Yugoslav dictator has suggested that Tito took a personal interest in the blackmail attempt against Waldheim. 'He loved such things,' he has said, referring to Tito's early years as a Comintern agent. 'Don't forget that Tito himself was involved in conspiratorial work.'[2] Mirko Milutinovic, Tito's long-time chief of staff, revealed, 'I knew that Waldheim had been compromised', implying that the Yugoslav dictator also knew. But Milutinovic added, 'Tito did not regard Waldheim as a war criminal'. A member of the dictator's entourage stated that Tito looked upon Waldheim as a 'Soviet man' who 'had likely ties to the United States'. Another former member of Tito's staff suggested that Tito viewed Waldheim as a 'convenient figure for the UN job', since he was a 'pliable' man.[3] Tito obviously realized that Waldheim was a puppet of the super-

1. Waldheim, *In the Eye of the Storm*, p. 125.
2. *Washington Post*, 30 October 1986.
3. Ibid.

powers, but he used the 1947 war crimes file to gain his own leverage over the pliable Secretary General.

Others have verified the testimony of Tito's aides who indicate that the Yugoslav dictator was aware of Waldheim's concealed past. The former Austrian Chancellor Bruno Kreisky has said that Tito knew about Waldheim's service on the staff of Army Group E but he was 'very cunning'. Mitja Ribicic, former Prime Minister of Slovenia and Yugoslavia, told an Austrian newspaper that Tito 'knew that Waldheim had been on the German front'. Ribicic added that if the dictator wasn't familiar with Waldheim's past then 'it certainly was known to people in his secretariat'.[1] Ribicic denied that the Yugoslavs used this information to blackmail Waldheim. It is inconceivable that if Tito's staff knew about Waldheim's past they could have kept this information from Tito. It is equally inconceivable that the Yugoslav dictator would not have used this information for his own benefit.

Mitja Ribicic is a key figure in the Waldheim story. His contact with Waldheim began in the 1940s when Ribicic served as deputy director of the Slovenian branch of Yugoslav state security. For many years when he was a high-ranking official in Slovenia and later as the Yugoslav Prime Minister, Ribicic may have had links with Waldheim on behalf of Marshal Tito. It is rumoured that Ribicic also helped Waldheim in support of the Alpa-Adrica movement which proposes a cultural union of Catholic Slovenia and Croatia with Austria, Italy and Catholic southern Germany.[2] (Waldheim's support for the political agenda of the Catholic Church must be kept in mind when considering the Pope's decision to meet the Austrian President.)

It is not known to what degree Tito was aware of

1. *Kurier* (Vienna), 20 April 1986.
2. Private information.

Waldheim's dealings with the separatist movement of Catholic Slovenia, but clearly Waldheim was playing a dangerous game since the Yugoslav dictator considered the Slovenian and Croatian separatists his bitterest opponents. However, Waldheim may have had an ace up his sleeve should Tito have considered exposing the Secretary General's hidden war crimes file. As an intelligence officer Waldheim had access to the documents showing that Tito had engaged in treasonable negotiations with the Germans in the Second World War.

Despite their intrigues, Waldheim and Tito had a great deal in common, particularly their mutual opposition to the Soviets. According to Waldheim, in their meetings Tito expressed 'a deep fear of the Russians, particularly after the 1968 Prague Spring liberation movement had been destroyed by Soviet forces'. Tito frequently lectured Waldheim on the danger which the USSR posed for Yugoslavia and Austria since he feared a possible 'Soviet threat through Austria and south to the Dalmatian coast'.[1]

Tito was also greatly worried that the movement of non-aligned nations, which he had helped to create, was falling under Soviet influence. Waldheim writes that the Yugoslav dictator 'was deeply concerned on how the non-aligned movement could maintain its credibility if Cuba with its close links to the Soviet Union was its leader'. By and large Waldheim and Tito co-operated. The Secretary General planned to make Belgrade a major UN centre, after New York and Geneva. More important, both Waldheim and Tito greatly favoured the *détente* policy of the 1970s. Thus it is not surprising that the Yugoslav dictator chose not to expose Waldheim's hidden UNWCC file.

There is evidence that other governments had knowledge of Waldheim's hidden past, including the French. Some of

1. Waldheim, *In the Eye of the Storm*, p. 125.

Waldheim's military records are in German archives in the French section of Berlin. In March 1979 the French military authorities in Berlin requested Waldheim's records and reported to Paris that his army service had not ended in Russia but had continued as a member of the staff of Army Group E.[1] At the same time the French also checked the American-controlled Berlin Document Centre which holds the Nazi party records showing that Waldheim had never applied for membership in the Nazi party and that he had not been a member of the SS or SA (students in the SA riding club apparently were not considered members of the SA).[2] The President of France in 1979, Valéry Giscard d'Estaing, and former Foreign Minister Jean-François Poncet have denied knowledge of the French reports on Waldheim made while he served as UN Secretary General. But it is difficult to believe that such information on a world leader like Waldheim was not passed to higher authorities. If the upper echelons of the Paris government did not already know about Waldheim's secret dossier, the next step would have been to check his name on all war crimes lists, including the UNWCC and CROWCASS, which were in the hands of the French.

There is also reason to believe that the West Germans were aware that Waldheim concealed his service in the Balkans. In September 1972 the West Berlin Interior Ministry requested Waldheim's records from the archives in the city.[3] This inquiry was probably made at the request of the Foreign Ministry in Bonn. The Austrians also requested the same records from the archives in Berlin. But Waldheim's hidden past was already well known to many people in the Vienna

1. *New York Times*, 5 June 1986.
2. Document 13 reveals that all inquiries about Waldheim's possible membership of Nazi organizations were answered in the negative.
3. *New York Times*, June 5, 1986.

government. From their intelligence contacts in Vienna in the 1940s and their knowledge of the records of the UN War Crimes Commission, which met in London, the British probably also knew about the false UNWCC file prepared against Waldheim for blackmail purposes. In view of Greece's membership of the UNWCC, Waldheim's service in that country in the Second World War, and the attitude of Ambassador Stravopoulos in 1980, it seems highly possible that Greece was among the countries that knew Waldheim's secret. It is likely that the decision to put Waldheim in as the puppet head of the UN was made by the superpowers acting alone – Israel, France, Yugoslavia and other countries probably learned about the Secretary General's hidden past subsequently.

Towards the end of Waldheim's ten-year service as Secretary General there were signs that *détente* between the superpowers was breaking down. Afghanistan was a principal area of tension between the USA and the USSR. The Soviet invasion of Afghanistan in December 1979 certainly put Kurt Waldheim, the creature of *détente*, in a difficult position. On 7 January 1980 a Security Council resolution calling for the withdrawal of all foreign troops from Afghanistan was vetoed by the Soviet Union. A week later the General Assembly passed a resolution deploring the occupation and asking the Secretary General to seek a solution through his good offices. Another resolution in November 1980 expressed a desire for a solution that would preserve the 'territorial sovereignty' and 'political independence' of Afghanistan. The resolution authorized Waldheim to appoint a special representative to mediate the crisis.

The Soviets took a tough line, opposing the General Assembly resolution and telling Waldheim that he was not required to appoint a mediator. In the spirit of a new Cold War the Americans naturally pressed Waldheim to appoint a prestigious mediator to put pressure on the Russians. 'One side tells me to implement the resolution,' a perplexed Waldheim told an interviewer. 'The other side says, "No, we don't want it." Of course I respect the General Assembly's wishes but I have to make sure my efforts to implement them will be constructive.' Caught between pressure from the Russians and the Third World supported by the Americans, Waldheim procrastinated, pointing out that after the Hungarian revolution of 1956 the UN had appointed a mediator but he had not been allowed into Hungary by the Russians. 'Is that really what the Assembly wants to happen in Afghanistan?' Answering his own question Waldheim added, 'of course not'.[1] Eventually Waldheim sent his aide Javier Perez de Cuellar to attempt to negotiate a Soviet withdrawal. Although he was not successful de Cuellar gained much favourable publicity.

In 1981 there was another election for Secretary General. Waldheim made it clear to all concerned that he wanted a third five-year term. In his memoirs he notes that he had the backing of the Soviet Ambassador Oleg Troyanovsky, who told him 'an old shoe fits better than a new one'.[2] The British and Americans also assured Waldheim of their support. President Reagan told Waldheim 'not to worry' about American support for his re-election bid. As usual the big problem for Waldheim was Communist China.

Peking regarded Waldheim as the 'American candidate' who also had Russian support. Like the Third World, the Chinese saw Waldheim as the pawn of the superpowers. The Americans urged the Chinese to vote for Waldheim. He notes: 'George Bush and Al Haig told me that when they had raised the question of my candidacy with Huang Hua, he had stonewalled.'

There was considerable support, particularly among Third

1. *New York Times*, (Magazine), 13 September 1981.
2. Waldheim, *In the Eye of the Storm*, p. 232.

World delegates, for Salim Ahmed Salim, the Foreign Minister of Tanzania. But the Americans made it clear that he was totally unacceptable. The cornerstone of American UN policy was never to allow Third World control of the United Nations. There was, however, a feeling that a non-European should be Secretary General. Since they could not have Kurt Waldheim, the superpowers agreed to accept his aide, Javier Perez de Cuellar, who had served as special UN representative on Afghanistan. The Peruvian diplomat has since been re-elected for a second term as Secretary General. As expected he had kept a low profile and resisted the initiatives of the Third World General Assembly.

Waldheim's service to the Americans did not end when he left the UN. In 1982, when the General Assembly was considering a censure motion against the USA on a charge of colonialism in Puerto Rico, the US mission to the UN 'sent out scouts to find Kurt Waldheim'.[1] According to a member of the US delegation to the UN, Waldheim was located 'somewhere on the lecture circuit' and instructed by the Americans to make sure the Austrian delegation voted the right way on the Puerto Rican issue, which was of great importance to the US government. The Austrian UN mission changed its attitude after Waldheim's intervention.

Former American ambassador to the UN, Daniel P. Moynihan, has been among those suggesting that Waldheim was an anti-American agent working for the KGB. Moynihan suspects Waldheim because he never tried to 'moderate the pro-Soviet position of the non-aligned'.[2] Although there is no basis for this accusation, charges that Waldheim was the enemy of Israel and the United States became quite common in the campaign against the Secretary General which began in March 1986.

1. Thomas M. Franck, *Nation Against Nation*, p. 201.
2. *New York Times*, 14 June 1986.

CHAPTER VI

The Campaign

'They all knew!' was my immediate thought on the evening of 24 March 1986 as I heard the announcement on the 6 p.m. news that Kurt Waldheim's name had been found on a CROWCASS list in the US National Archives. Most astonishing was the revelation that there was a cross-reference on the CROWCASS list to a dossier on Waldheim in the UNWCC files. A spokesman for the UN told reporters that they were searching their archives seeking to locate Waldheim's dossier among the records of the UN War Crimes Commission.

Six years before, people in Washington and New York had suggested to me that Waldheim had a negative attitude toward war crimes investigations. I believed that Waldheim was trying to protect his cronies in Austria. But it had never occurred to me in 1980 that the man being covered up in record group 30 was the Secretary General himself. Although I had not been able to discover the truth, I had always felt that the secret contained in the UNWCC files would eventually become public. I saved all my information on record group 30 for the day I was sure would come when the world would be talking about the person or persons covered up in the UNWCC files.

In the autumn of 1985 Waldheim had attended an official dinner where he met Hans Janachek, a fellow Austrian who had served under him at the UN. Janachek was surprised when the usually formal Waldheim addressed him in the familiar '*Du*' form for the first time. The reason for the former Secretary General's friendly tone soon became clear.

Since he planned to run for President of Austria as the

candidate of the People's Party, Waldheim told his former subordinate, 'you know, Hans, your friends the Socialists are already starting their attacks'.[1] Janachek, who had a position of influence in the Austrian Socialist Party, realized that Waldheim – who considered himself a national hero – wanted help to avoid the usual campaign scrutiny. When Janachek reminded Waldheim, 'you have to expect criticism in an election', the former Secretary General stormed out of the room. Janachek later realized that Waldheim feared that his past would be exposed.

There were many in Austria who already knew about Waldheim's service in Yugoslavia. Indeed, after his return to Vienna from his tenure at the UN, Waldheim gave considerable information on the Balkan theatre to the author of a book on General Löhr and another researcher writing a history of modern Austria.[2] Waldheim's 'hidden past' in Yugoslavia was common knowledge to most people in Vienna familiar with the history of Austria's role in the Second World War, as well as many in government and diplomatic service. At about the same time in early March 1986 as the information on his student affiliation was published in Austria, Waldheim's military record was revealed. But revelation of Waldheim's name on the CROWCASS and UNWCC lists caused the greatest stir.

On the morning of 25 March 1986 I read the *New York Times* story about the discovery of the CROWCASS list at the National Archives. The article mentioned the UNWCC files but made no reference to my experiences six years earlier. Robert Rosenstock, the legal counsel of the US mission to the United Nations told the *New York Times* that, in 1980, American officials had been able 'to see what we wanted to see' in

1. Interview with Hans Janachek.
2. *Profil*, 1 April 1986, and confidential source.

the UN archives. But Alan Ryan who in 1980 had headed the Justice Department's Office of Special Investigations (OSI) stated that the UN had refused to provide 'blanket access' to the war crimes files. Neal Sher, the current head of OSI, claimed that as recently as 1984 his office had been denied the right 'to search through the United Nations files'. Both Ryan and Sher implied that OSI did not have the CROW-CASS and UNWCC list of names (Ryan had informed me in 1980 that OSI had the UNWCC list, a fact confirmed by a researcher in 1985).

After reading the *New York Times* article, I made some inquiries and discovered that it was Eli Rosenbaum of the World Jewish Congress who claimed to have found Waldheim's name on the CROWCASS list. I became suspicious when I learned that Rosenbaum had worked as an attorney for OSI. Could he have learned about the presence of Waldheim's name on the CROWCASS and UNWCC lists while he was employed by the Justice Department?

I called Rosenbaum just before he was about to preside at a news conference. He seemed rather cordial until I confronted him with the fact that OSI had the CROWCASS list in 1980. Rosenbaum admitted that OSI had the early CROWCASS lists, but according to him the Justice Department didn't have the eighteenth and final list which had Waldheim's name on it. This seemed strange since the early CROWCASS lists were highly perishable mimeograph sheets that are very rare, while the eighteenth list, which contains Waldheim's name, is a permanent printed pamphlet which has 'Destroy all previous lists' marked on it.

Rosenbaum was called to testify at a congressional hearing on Waldheim. Unfortunately he was not asked directly, while under oath, when he had learned that the former Secretary General was on the CROWCASS list. Later I spoke to several congressional staffers who made it clear that not a

single member of Congress thought it possible that the US
government could have been unaware of Waldheim's hidden
past.

It seemed important to me to get my story of what had
occurred in 1980 told to Congress but I suspected that this
would not be easy since I implicated Israel in the cover-up of
Waldheim. It has been alleged that Congress tends to be the
most pro-Zionist institution in the USA, more so perhaps
than the news media or even the universities. In 1986 I found
out just how much influence the Zionist lobby had in
Washington.

A friend told me that he knew an aide to a member of the
congressional committee investigating the Waldheim matter.
The Washington staffer seemed very interested when he
learned that I had been the one who discovered the UN war
crimes files in 1980. However, he lost enthusiasm when he
was informed my testimony would implicate Israel in the
cover-up of Waldheim and the UN war crimes files. 'Don't
you realize,' the aide told my friend, 'the Congressman has
good relations with the Jewish community.' I never received
an invitation to testify before the committee investigating the
Waldheim affair.

Somewhat later I was called by a former congressional
staffer whom I had met in 1980. He still had many contacts in
Washington and he offered to help me get my 1980 experiences publicized. As a devout Zionist he saw the story of a
cover-up of the UNWCC files as a good way of discrediting
the UN. However, when I described my contacts with the
Israeli mission to the UN in 1980, he kept repeating 'I have a
problem with that.' He said 'I know from 1980 that you are an
honest guy and you are probably right about Israel knowing
about Waldheim. But I just can't do anything against Israel.' I
never heard from him again. I spoke to several other people
who informed me that neither the American press nor

Congress would give any publicity to the story of the cover-up of Waldheim by Israel. Ironically there was some interest in my testimony of a cover-up of the former Secretary General by the CIA and the Justice Department. It was somewhat disturbing to realize that the press and Congress were more afraid to explore the transgressions of a foreign country than those of their own government.

During the Austrian election the American press told the Waldheim story from a perspective that was highly favourable to Israel. Prime Minister Shimon Perez denied that Israel had any files on the former Secretary General – a story which was carried by the American press without comment. The Israelis appeared indignant about the UN files and Waldheim's military record despite their long-standing knowledge of both.

The Israeli ambassador to the UN visited the archives to see the Waldheim dossier, and the event was widely reported in the American news media to portray the Israelis as the injured party seeking justice for the victims of the Holocaust. But the newspapers neglected to mention that in four decades Israel had carried out only two war crimes trials or that in the 1950s it had agreed to forgo war crimes investigations in exchange for West German reparation payments (see page 95).

Despite their own dubious record, the Israelis attempted to use the UNWCC issue to discredit the UN because of its frequent anti-Zionist positions. On 24 April the *New York Times* reported that the Israelis were requesting access to the archives to obtain the files on hundreds of Nazi war criminals. The Israelis claimed that they had never obtained any of the numerous copies of the UNWCC register of 40,000 names so that they had to ask a 'friendly government' to let them see a copy of the list. The *New York Times* noted that 'the United States had a copy of the master list'. Remarkably this crucial fact was buried in the *New York Times* story.

Anyone familiar with Israeli–American intelligence relations cannot conceive that anything like a war crimes list
could be kept from the Israelis for so many decades. One
American intelligence expert was asked in 1981 about the
operation of Mossad. 'They have penetrated all through the
US government,' he replied. An official of the US State
Department (which had a copy of the UNWCC list) was
quoted as saying, 'I urged several times that the US quit
trying to keep secrets from Israel. Let them have everything.
They always get what they want anyway.'[1] CIA reports
indicate that Mossad has a thorough network which had
completely penetrated all departments of the US government.

The Israeli penetration of the US mission to the UN was
particularly thorough. Former US ambassador to the UN
Andrew Young recalls: 'I operated on the assumption that the
Israelis would learn everything instantly. I just always
assumed that everything was monitored and that there was a
pretty formal network.'[2] Mossad is also very active in the UN
Secretariat. In 1980, Ambassador Rosenne told me that Israel
had obtained information from the UN archives. Not all his
statements were correct but in view of the lax security at the
archives, he would appear to be right on this point. It is quite
possible that for many years the Israelis not only had the list of
names but copies of the actual UNWCC files.

In April 1986 the US news media failed to undertake any
investigation of the Israeli role in the UN scandal but instead
they accepted the Israeli version of events without question.
Typical was the focus of attention on the Israeli demand that
the UN supply the files of Alois Brunner, a Nazi war criminal
believed to be in Syria. It was of course no coincidence that
the Israelis publicized the one Nazi in an Arab country while

1. *Newsweek*, 3 September 1979.
2. Paul Findley, *They Dare to Speak Out*, p. 148.

ignoring the many war criminals who had worked for NATO, the CIA and the West German government.[1]

In spring 1986 the major press focus was on Waldheim, who played into the hands of the WJC. Instead of giving an honest account of his service in the Balkans, the former Secretary General compounded his appearance of guilt by denying that he knew about the deportation of Greek Jews to Auschwitz. Waldheim's inconsistent responses to questions about Kozara and other areas where atrocities were committed made the WJC allegations seem substantive. The People's Party candidate lost all credibility with the American and European press, but in his own country Waldheim gained a great deal of sympathy because of the attacks against him.

Indeed, as early as 10 March Peter Michael Lingens accurately predicted the course of the election campaign. According to the Vienna journalist, all older Austrians who made compromises during the Nazi period would be happy to find out that Waldheim is a 'human being just like you and me'. A spokesman for the Socialist party commented on Waldheim's student affiliations, 'that he was with the Nazis could help him, that he denies it could harm him'.

Lingens saw that the anti-Semites in Austria would take advantage of the attacks on Waldheim, particularly since the WJC were guilty of making charges that were 'greatly exaggerated'. The Vienna journalist believed all Austrians would unite behind Waldheim in rage against the world's antagonism, particularly since the anti-Semites would claim that 'our poor little country is the victim of the Jewish-dominated world press'.[2] Indeed, Otto Scrinzi – the far-right candidate for Austrian President – who originally had little support gained

1. See Chapter III for UNWCC suspects living in West Germany.
2. *Profil*, 16 March 1987.

considerable strength because of the Waldheim controversy.

Waldheim changed his campaign strategy. Ironically he had begun by describing himself as 'the man whom the whole world trusted'. After the revelations about his past he portrayed himself as an innocent victim of a smear campaign. All other issues in the campaign were soon forgotten. What resulted was a referendum on Kurt Waldheim and in a larger sense a vote of confidence on Austria's past.

In the *New York Times* on 3 May Israeli Foreign Minister (now Prime Minister) Yitzhak Shamir blasted Waldheim and urged Austrians to refrain from voting for him as president. 'It will be a tragic fact that such a man will be elected to such a position,' he lamented. Shamir took the opportunity to charge that the Arabs had collaborated with the Nazis. 'All the Arab leaders at the time of the Second World War were great admirers of Hitler.' Shamir failed to note his own record in the war – which was far worse than Waldheim's or that of any Arab.

Among Shamir's crimes is complicity in the brutal murder of the UN envoy Count Bernadotte in 1948, which he has admitted. During the Second World War the Stern Gang, to which Shamir belonged, had even offered an alliance with Nazi Germany to gain Hitler's aid in expelling the British from Palestine; Shamir and his Stern Gang colleagues wished to replace them with a 'quisling Jewish government' as a satellite of the 'new Germany'. David Rubinstein, the Israeli journalist, notes that in 1941 the Stern Gang rejoiced at every Nazi victory and British defeat.[1] They even had plans to raise a contingent to help the Nazis fight the British in North Africa!

In July 1986 Professor Leibowitz compared Shamir's record to Waldheim's. Leibowitz noted that Israel would not send an ambassador to Vienna because of the election of

1. *Middle East International*, 10 October 1986.

Waldheim, 'but we will accept as prime minister a person who led an organization which offered its services to Hitler'. Leibowitz correctly pointed out that 'Waldheim was mobilized into Hitler's army and did his duty there', but the Stern Gang 'was not mobilized into Hitler's army and yet its members volunteered themselves to serve Hitler'.[1] Such valid observations can be made in the Israeli press but no American publication would have the courage to publish them.

On 6 May 1986 I held a press conference at the UN. The atmosphere was considerably different from the press conference six years earlier. To avoid giving me credibility the *New York Times* was conspicuously absent,[2] and many of the UN reporters, especially the Americans, were openly hostile to my suggestion that Israel and the US Justice Department had been involved in the cover-up of Waldheim and the UNWCC files. However, there was some comic relief at the press conference. Just before I began my presentation, I was approached by a radio journalist who was well known as a staunch supporter of Israel. He told me that he wanted me on his show and said that his assistant was setting up in the next room where he would interview me after the press conference. Realizing that he would never allow me on his programme with a story so embarrassing to Israel, I asked him to read my press release before making any arrangement for an interview. 'Oh don't worry,' he said, 'I have been following the Waldheim story and I want everyone connected with it on my show.'

Walking away, the radio reporter raised his eyebrows as he

---

1. *Yidrot Aharonot*, 18 July 1986.
2. Although no reporter from the *New York Times* attended, a transcript of the press conference was contained in the newspaper's 'Palumbo File', which was shown to me by someone who had obviously been given a copy as a reward for providing information. Such is the Byzantine intrigue typical of the Waldheim affair.

read my press release indicating an Israeli cover-up of Waldheim. Suddenly he ran to the next room to cancel the taping session. I later found out that he had called the Public Broadcasting Network to make sure that I could not appear on any of its programmes. When the Zionist reporter returned to the press conference, he and a few like-minded colleagues made numerous taunts, including the suggestion that I had been paid to make statements embarrassing to Israel. The truth was of course that my revelations about the Israeli cover-up of Waldheim prevented me from receiving credit in the USA for having discovered the UNWCC files six years earlier.

In fact there were numerous editorials and articles which asked why no one had investigated the UNWCC files while Waldheim was secretary general. When I spoke to American journalists and informed them about my experiences in 1980, usually they were anxious to do a story about me until they learned that Israel was involved in the Waldheim cover-up. It has been claimed that it is harder to get bad news about Israel published in the USA than in Israel. This was certainly true in my case since I was able to get an article about my discovery of the UNWCC files in an Israeli news magazine but not in a single American publication. On 13 May 1986 the London *Times* ran a substantial story on the leader page entitled 'Waldheim: a question mark over Israel', which was based on my testimony. It was written by Keith Hindell of the BBC, who in 1980 had helped me in my attempt to solve the UNWCC mystery.

In 1980 the *New York Times* reported my discovery of the UNWCC files. In 1986 I was interviewed by a *New York Times* journalist who said he wanted to do a follow-up story on me but, as in so many other cases, he lost interest when I told him Israel was involved in the cover-up of Kurt Waldheim. This was in fact common knowledge. One European journalist told

me that a high-ranking official of the World Jewish Congress
told him that Israel could be among the countries which
covered-up Waldheim, while a second WJC official told
another European journalist 'off the record' that Israel definitely had Waldheim's files while he was Secretary General.[1]

On 16 May the *New York Times*, which refused to do a story
about the Israeli cover-up of Waldheim, published a rebuttal
to the London *Times* story. It decried the unnamed person
who claimed 'a conspiracy theory that countries may have
discovered Mr Waldheim's background when he first ran for
secretary general'. The Israeli ambassador to the UN, Benjamin Netanyahu, who apparently inspired the article, said
that he 'assumed that the record of Mr Waldheim, a former
Austrian Foreign Minister, had to be clean'. The *New York
Times* article tried to give the impression that most UN diplomats did not believe that there had been a cover-up of
Waldheim's past. In reality, just as in the US congress, few if
any diplomats believed it possible that Waldheim could have
kept his service in Yugoslavia secret from the CIA and KGB.
Ambassador Netanyahu's remarks put the Israelis squarely on
the side of those trying to discourage a serious investigation of
the Waldheim affair.

The *New York Times* suggested that in 1971, when
Waldheim was being considered for secretary general, no one
bothered to look up his 'personal background'. Of course,
there was a thorough investigation of every candidate for
secretary general. It is impossible to believe that Waldheim's
background would be unchecked, since at the very least
everyone knew that he had served in the Wehrmacht in

1. A book written from a WJC perspective notes that Israeli Justice Minister
Yitzhak Modai 'hinted several times that Israel knew about Kurt Waldheim's
past'. There is also scepticism about UN ambassador Yehuda Blum's claim 'to
have been unaware of his Nazi past or even the existence of the United Nations
files': Rosenzweig and Cohen, *Waldheim*, pp. 126, 159.

Russia. With such a background every war crimes list would have been consulted in 1971 by the KGB and CIA as well as Mossad, to see what they had on Waldheim in the highly unlikely event that they did not already know about his service in Yugoslavia. The *New York Times* refutation of my story of the cover-up of Waldheim in 1980 while he was secretary general reminded me of the Soviet Union, where dissidents are denounced without their names or their views being published.

Ironically, on 14 May the *New York Times* had published an article which made it obvious that many countries had to know about Waldheim's military record. In Suitland, Maryland, in an annexe to the National Archives, the register of 40,000 names in the UNWCC files was discovered. As we have seen, hundreds of copies of this master index were distributed to seventeen different member governments.

The chief focus in the spring of 1986 was of course on the Austrian presidential election. But while Waldheim and his Socialist opponent, Dr Kurt Steyrer, carried on their some-times heated contest, at a press conference on 25 March Israel Singer of the WJC declared: 'Our first accusation is that Kurt Waldheim is a Nazi. He was unfit to serve as Secretary General of the United Nations.'[1] Singer added: 'We are not interested in any election other than his election as Secretary General of the UN.'

The chief aim of the WJC was not in exposing what they called 'a proven Nazi' but in discrediting the international organization over which he had served as chief executive. This appeal hit a responsive chord in the American pro-Israel Jewish community, which since the 1975 anti-Zionist resolution had sought a way of getting back at the UN. After the

1. WJC press release.

revelations about Waldheim were first made the idea that he had been a sponsor of the 1975 General Assembly resolution spread like wildfire among pro-Zionist Jews in America.

On 25 April 1986 an article in the *Jewish Press* by David Horowitz expressed what despite a total lack of evidence had already become the accepted dogma. According to the anti-UN correspondent, 'Waldheim found something in common with Yasser Arafat who together with his murderous PLO found some comfort and even glory under the Waldheim canopy. It was under this canopy that the pro-PLO Secretariat unit with its many offshoots emerged.'

An article in the *Jewish Times* on 17 July 1986, which called Waldheim 'the Soviet's UN man', expressed the feeling of many American Zionists. It was alleged that Waldheim 'encouraged the PLO and welcomed its bully-boy Arafat to the General Assembly'. The former Secretary General was also condemned because he had been 'overseer of a situation where Lebanon was sacrificed to Syria (a Russian satrapy) and Afghanistan fell to Soviet conquest without organized individual protest'. But Waldheim was most seriously attacked because 'during his administration the obscene "Zionism is racism" resolution was passed by an alliance of Communist and Arab anti-Semitic networks followed by a routinized series of anti-Semitic and anti-Israeli outbreaks every week or two for years'. According to the *Jewish Times* Waldheim had become Secretary General by a 'Soviet power play'.

The fact that this type of analysis of Waldheim's tenure as UN chief was totally irrational did not diminish its appeal. Clearly many Zionists wanted to believe that Waldheim was a Nazi who acted as an agent for the Soviets and PLO. Another goal of the WJC campaign against Waldheim was to force Austria to face its Nazi past. But the WJC were irresponsible in the threats they made against the Austrian people should

Waldheim be elected. The Secretary General of the WJC, Israel Singer, promised that with Waldheim as president 'the next few years will not be easy for the Austrians'.[1] Singer made it clear that the WJC had long-term plans: 'Do you think we'll pull back from Waldheim after the election? It will go on. In the whole world it will be said that a former Nazi and a liar is the representative of Austria. Everybody with an Austrian passport will have this cloud of uncertainty travel with him.' Ivan Hacker-Lederer, the president of Vienna's Jewish community, criticized Singer's remarks which he believed 'improved Waldheim's electoral chances'.

Simon Wiesenthal, the world-famous war crimes investigator, was another critic of the WJC. He told the press: 'Do you know what is reviving anti-Semitism here? It is not revelations about Waldheim's past. No, it is an interview by Israel Singer of the World Jewish Congress telling Austrians that Bitburg[2] was one bitter day for President Reagan and that if Austrians elect Waldheim, the population of Austria is going to get six years of Bitburg.' Wiesenthal made it clear that the WJC had no case against Waldheim. The Nazi-hunter criticized the former UN Secretary General for denying he knew about the deportations of Jews, but he stated that there was no evidence indicating that Waldheim was a war criminal – had he been, Wiesenthal would have exposed him decades ago.

In a number of interviews Wiesenthal explained his views on the Waldheim affair:[3] the WJC had 'demonized' the former UN Secretary General because 'there is a kind of hysteria over Waldheim in America'. But Wiesenthal stood firm,

1. *New York Times*, 28 April 1986.
2. President Reagan's visit to an SS cemetery, which caused a storm of protest by Jewish and other groups.
3. *Christian Science Monitor*, 24 June 1986; *Jewish Exponent*, 7 November 1986; *Jewish Times*, 13 November 1986.

saying: 'I can't kill a reputation of forty years over a burst of hysteria.' He added: 'I find that to accuse someone of being a war criminal, a murderer, without evidence is not in accordance with Jewish ethics.'

Wiesenthal correctly pointed out that the WJC 'has made people believe that Waldheim was one of the biggest war criminals'. But to him, 'Waldheim is a false symbol of the Nazis. He is a liar and an opportunist but he never was a member of the Nazi party. And there is no evidence that he was an assassin or a leader of the deportation of Jews.' Wiesenthal also blamed the WJC for trying to convince people that Waldheim was responsible for 'Austrian and UN policies hostile to Israel and the Jews'. His biggest complaint against the WJC was that they made 'collective threats against all of Austria and this is not in accordance with Jewish ethics'.

It is difficult to evaluate the degree to which the Waldheim affair has increased anti-Semitism in Austria. In an interview (*Jewish Week*, 28 August 1987) Waldheim claimed that there is no more anti-Semitism in Austria than in other countries. He points to a survey which indicates that only 7 per cent of Austrians have anti-Semitic attitudes, adding: 'No Jews have been attacked physically by Austrian by-passers. On the contrary, there are friendly feelings.' But the fact that there are no *pogroms* on the streets of Vienna is hardly sufficient assurance that Austria's ancient tradition of anti-Semitism is dead. Despite the 'quantitative analysis' of 'social scientists', there is no really accurate way to measure the degree of anti-Semitism in any country. It is hard to believe that people would respond honestly on such a sensitive subject. Not surprisingly, recent surveys have yielded contradictory results, perhaps reflecting the bias of their sponsors.

The poll referred to by Waldheim was conducted by the Austrian Joint Group for Information and Media Research. It compared attitudes in Austria in the summer of 1986 to a similar survey taken in June 1985 before the Waldheim affair. Dr Heinz Kierzl, a Viennese Jew, who served as director of the Austrian National Bank attempted to publicize this survey, which is highly favourable to Austria, in America.[1] The poll indicated that in 1985 10 per cent of Austrians would refuse to shake hands with a Jew, but in the summer of 1986 the figure was 7 per cent. There was a drop from 7 per cent to 5 per cent of Austrians who believed that the Jews had been a negative influence on culture and civilization. According to Dr Kierzl, the only increase, from 3 per cent to 4 per cent, was of those who felt that Austria would be better off without the Jews. But it is hard to believe that overall anti-Semitism has actually decreased in Austria in the wake of the Waldheim affair. It is probable that people in Austria have become more aware that the whole world is watching their reaction to surveys on anti-Semitism and that it is best to hide their true feelings. Indeed, another survey on anti-Semitism in Austria yields a completely different result.

'The floodgates have been opened', according to Maxmillian Gottschlich, a non-Jewish professor at the University of Vienna. His survey indicates:

... the proportion of Austrians who believe Jews have an aversion to hard work rose to 39 per cent after Waldheim's election from 32 per cent in 1980. During the same period, the percentage of those who believe Jews possessed too much economic power rose from 32 per cent to 39 per cent. In 1980, 33 per cent believed Jews had too much economic and political influence, but in 1986 the figure rose to 48 per cent.[2]

The study, conducted in July 1986, showed that 16 per cent of Austrians believed that their country of seven million would be better off without its 8,000 Jews while 38 per cent

1. *Jewish Times*, 21 October 1986; *Jewish Exponent*, 31 October 1986.
2. *Jewish Week*, 3 April 1987.

felt that Jews themselves were partly responsible for their frequent persecutions in the past. Professor Gottschlich believes 'a climate has been created in which it is now possible to speak openly against Jews' in Austria.

The worst example of this occurred when Karl Hödl, deputy mayor of Linz, sent a letter in May 1986 to Edgar Bronfman, president of the WJC: 'you Jews got Christ but you're not going to get Waldheim the same way', the Austrian official wrote. Former US ambassador in Vienna, Ronald S. Lauder, pointed out: 'The deputy mayor of Linz would not have lasted fifteen minutes any other place in the Western world. He is still in office today.'[1] Lauder believes that there is a great deal of anti-Semitism in present-day Austria. 'They feel envy for anyone who is successful. They feel that the Jewish people have always been successful.' Of course the WJC's attacks on an Austrian national hero during the presidential election played into the hands of anti-Semites.

Since the Austrian election the Israeli government has campaigned to 'open up' the UNWCC files. In fact, during spring 1986, the UN legal office had announced that the UN files were available to member governments upon request, to be used for legitimate purposes on a confidential basis. Hundreds of files were given to Israel. Therefore in 1986 the UN conformed with the original intentions of the War Crimes Commission as well as finally granting the request I had made in 1980. The Israeli demand that the files be opened up unconditionally to the general public was questionable since there is a danger in releasing information that may be unintentionally inaccurate. It must also be realized that Waldheim was not the only person against whom a false file was prepared for purposes of blackmail. Informants in Yugoslavia

1. *New York Times*, 9 October 1987. He was rather belatedly removed from office.

made it clear that dozens of others were targeted by the Tito government for blackmail in this way. Other countries also used UNWCC dossiers for political and espionage purposes.

The real goal of the Israeli campaign to open the UNWCC files to the general public was to embarrass the UN, which surely would resist such a demand and could thus be portrayed by the Israelis as 'anti-Semitic'. Because of the anti-Zionist positions taken by the UN, the Israelis have long sought a way of discrediting the organization.

The Israelis, who usually portrayed themselves as avengers of the Holocaust, have in reality done almost nothing to apprehend Nazis, and for decades have participated in a gentleman's agreement to keep the files closed. These obvious inconsistencies have not prevented the Zionists from exploiting the UNWCC issue. Gideon Hausner's successor as director of Yad Vashem, Yitzhak Arad, declared, 'the archives of the United Nations War Crimes Commission include material of the highest importance.[1] Arad mentioned the names of several Nazis listed by the UNWCC, including Goering, Goebbels and Mengele. All were of course safely dead. Conspicuously missing was the name of any suspect who had worked for West Germany, the CIA or NATO.

Arad claimed that the Waldheim case made the Israelis 'aware of the potential information contained in the files'. According to Arad: 'We knew that there was an archive in the United Nations for the War Crimes Commission. We were unaware of the amount of material there.' Arad did not of course mention that I gave a copy of the UNWCC index to his predecessor Gideon Hausner, who assured me that Yad Vashem was well aware of the UN war crimes files. Indeed, most of the Jewish community was not quite satisfied with the

1. *New York Times*, 20 May 1986.

Israeli explanation and propaganda campaign over the UNWCC files. The *Jewish Week* noted, 'for many the real question is how and why this vital source of information on Nazi war crimes went unnoticed for four decades.[1] No Zionist openly asked how it was possible Israel could have obtained the UNWCC files on Eichmann in 1960 without knowing about the nature of the UN war crimes records.

The UN Secretary General referred the matter of the UNWCC files to the original seventeen members of the War Crimes Commission. In March 1987 all except Australia agreed that the files should be available to member governments for war crimes investigations but that the information was too raw to be released to the general public. Besides, no case had been legally determined on the basis of the data in the files. Many of the people listed probably had no idea they were included in a war crimes archive. Despite the substantive arguments for not opening the UNWCC files to the general public, many have given automatic support to the Israeli demand for unconditional access to record group 30.[2] The Israelis have attempted to make it seem that the UN Secretariat rather than the former Commission members (including the USA) was responsible for the decision not to open the secret portions of the UNWCC files to the general public. Israeli Ambassador Benjamin Netanyahu claimed 'it is inconceivable for the United Nations to continue shielding accused Nazi war criminals.[3] The Israelis claimed that the 300 dossiers they had obtained for the UNWCC files

1. *Jewish Week*, 15 May 1987.
2. Ironically these were generally the same people who supported the Justice Department's decision to keep secret its report on Kurt Waldheim even though a judgement had been rendered to the world in the case and despite the irate demands of the Austrian government, including Waldheim himself, that the 200-page report be made public!
3. *New York Times*, 20 March 1987.

contained important information 'both for future prosecution and historical research'.

Several days later the right-wing *New York Post* carried a headline: 'Israelis track Nazi killers using secret UN files'. The story claimed that, 'on the basis of the files, Israel has launched a global hunt for the war criminals involved'.[1] The Israelis had in fact no intention of doing in the late 1980s what they had neglected to do for four decades.

The Israelis received considerable support in their campaign to use the UNWCC to discredit the UN. The Brooklyn District Attorney, Elizabeth Holtzman, charged the UN with a 'cover-up' because the organization refused to 'allow public disclosure of the files of suspected Nazi war criminals'.[2] But in 1980 I had offered Holtzman a chance to do something about the files while Waldheim was still Secretary General.

Holtzman, an American news media celebrity because of her role in the women's movement and the Watergate hearings, is also well known for her investigation of Nazi war criminals while she was a member of Congress. In 1980 she was a candidate for the US Senate and so she agreed to attend my press conference of 28 March 1980 to demand that the UN make the war crimes files available to member governments, which was my request at that time. Quite properly Holtzman made a check of my reliability at the City University and was given a favourable reference. I was told she would make 'other inquiries' about the UNWCC records.

In any case she never appeared at my 1980 press conference and her staff would not co-operate with my efforts to make the UN files available to member governments. When a mutual friend approached her about the UN files she became

1. *New York Post*, 24 March 1987.
2. *New York Daily News* (Brooklyn Section), 23 March 1987.

angry. We could not understand why she was so indifferent to my efforts in 1980 to open up the UN archives, which could have been a good issue in the New York primary for US Senate, where the electorate was largely Jewish. It is of course possible that she had made inquiries at the US or Israeli UN missions and was warned off. Whatever the reason it is most unfortunate that Holtzman never supported my efforts in 1980 since, with her celebrity status, she could have focused significant attention on the UNWCC records when it could have done some good. Holtzman's support of the Israeli 1987 initiative to open up the files unconditionally to the general public seemed like a demand for too much – too late.

Simon Wiesenthal had also lost an opportunity in 1980 to help open up the UNWCC files while Waldheim was still in office. Seven years later this did not stop Rabbi Marvin Heir, director of the Los Angeles Wiesenthal Center, from denouncing the decision to bar the general public from gaining access to the UNWCC files as an 'outrage'.[1] No Zionist seemed concerned about the real outrage – the Israeli failure to pursue serious war crimes investigations for four decades, and the efforts of the Jewish state to politicize the war crimes issue.

A. M. Rosenthal, Associate Editor of the *New York Times*, supported the Israeli effort to embarrass the UN over the UNWCC issue. In a column entitled 'The locked files', Rosenthal made several factual errors, including the claim that the 1987 UN policy on record group 30 'runs counter to the original intention of the Commission' because the files were not open to the general public. This is not true. Lord Wright and Dr Litawski never intended the sensitive portions of the UNWCC files to be open to historians and

1. *New York Post*, 24 March 1987.

journalists, but only to member governments for war crimes investigations which the UN was finally doing.

Rosenthal's statement that 'the protection of the innocent argument is moot' is also incorrect since there is evidence that Waldheim was not the only person to be blackmailed by Yugoslavia with a false UNWCC file. Considering the procedure of the UNWCC, it is also clear that many of the files are inaccurate. Opening the files to the general public without some protection for those listed would be unjust.

In the *New York Times* on 12 April 1987 the Israeli ambassador to the UN, Benjamin Netanyahu, again demanded that the sensitive portions of record group 30 be opened to the general public. He insisted that it was not the vote of the seventeen members of the Commission but the Secretary General who was keeping the records closed. 'It can be reversed by the Secretary General,' Netanyahu claimed.

Besides seeking to discredit the UN and cover up their own inaction, the Israelis tried to use their campaign over the UNWCC files to propagate the Zionist view of the Holocaust. This thesis holds that the British and Americans bear major responsibility for the annihilation of the Jews because London and Washington knew what was being done in Nazi-occupied Europe but the Allies refused to do anything. Such an interpretation ignores the fact that the quasi-governmental Zionist Jewish Agency in Palestine had over 30,000 men under arms during the Second World War but failed to make an effort to rescue the six million Jews being consumed in Europe. The Israeli claim that opening the UNWCC files to historians would make clear 'who knew what during the Holocaust' would appear highly doubtful.

The *New York Times* continued to give a large amount of coverage to the Israeli campaign to 'open up' the UN war crimes files to the general public. An article on Sunday 11 October 1987 by Ambassador Netanyahu gave many of the standard distortions on the UNWCC files used by the Israeli government. Netanyahu denied the UN's assertions that many war crimes files contain 'unproven rumours against innocent people'. According to the ambassador, 'the Commission which compiled the Nazi war crimes archives did not deal in "rumours". Its panel of eminent jurists recommended prosecution only in those 25,000 cases where solid evidence was produced.'

But Netanyahu is contradicted by Ambassador Shabtai Rosenne, the leading expert on war crimes in the Israeli Foreign Office, who indicated that the UNWCC files contain nothing more than 'suspicions and unproven accusations'.[1] This is an exaggeration, but some people were listed by the UNWCC even though the Commission could only approximate their name, while in other cases entire organization sheets of certain staffs were placed on the register without any evidence against particular individuals. As we have seen, Waldheim was included in the UNWCC list on the word of two German POWs, held in 're-education camps' in Communist Yugoslavia, whose testimony was changed to make it seem more incriminating.

Netanyahu also claimed that 'the opening of the archives is indispensable for a full understanding of the Holocaust'. There is nothing new, however, in the UNWCC records about the Holocaust. It is political propaganda to claim that the UN war crimes files contain mountains of new information, 'meticulously documented by the Allies during the World War II when it was possible to save millions'.

Ambassador Netanyahu believes that Israel's campaign on the UNWCC records is important since 'opening the archives to public scrutiny will compel reluctant governments to act'. But of all the governments concerned, Israel has done the

1. *Koteret Rashit*, 21 May 1986.

least on the war crimes problem. If the files were made available for publication, it is clear that the Zionists will simply continue their usual practice of using war crimes information for political purposes.

As a creature of the Zionist lobby, the Justice Department's Office of Special Investigation dutifully supported the Israeli campaign to 'open up' the UNWCC files. A few days after Netanyahu's article, OSI announced that it 'has for the first time used the archives of the United Nations War Crimes Commission to track down and charge an American accused of war crimes'. Peter Quintus, a former concentration camp guard in Poland who went to the USA in 1945, was supposedly apprehended based on material in the UNWCC archives. The Justice Department had the UNWCC list since 1980 – it seems quite a coincidence that just when the Israeli agitation over the UNWCC was reaching its peak, OSI made a case which 'clearly strengthens the Israeli argument that full access to the files will lead to more such prosecutions'.[1]

The *New York Times* and other news media identified France as the country which opposed making the UN files available to the general public. A spokesman for the French UN mission noted that the UNWCC files were 'like raw police files' and so 'real violations could occur if they are made public'. But such common sense had no impact. The French UN mission was bombarded by thousands of calls and telegrams demanding that its government stop trying to protect Nazi criminals. The French spokesman noted: 'It is difficult to rationally discuss an issue with people who are reacting in a highly emotional manner.'[2] Indeed, one caller on a radio chat show indicated he would boycott French

1. *New York Times*, 15 October 1987.
2. *Jewish Week*, 16 October 1987.

bread until the Paris government changed its attitude on the UNWCC files!

The agitation over the UNWCC files was fuelled by some rather irresponsible journalism. Typical was a story in the *Chicago Sun Times* on 18 October 1987 by the anti-UN correspondent Chuck Ashman, who actually wrote: 'In a locked box behind locked doors in a UN office building in New York are some 185 documents labelled "Kurt Waldheim – murder and other crimes".' Ashman's article gives the totally erroneous impression that there is a huge file on Waldheim in the UNWCC records that is being kept from the public. In reality there were only three or four pages on Waldheim in the UN archives, which had been made public in 1986. It is because of such reporting that concern in the Jewish community over Waldheim and the UNWCC files has reached the point of hysteria.

As has been seen, while the Israeli government was attempting to discredit the UN over the War Crimes Commission files, the World Jewish Congress were conducting their own campaign to prove that former Secretary General Kurt Waldheim was, in the words of WJC president Edgar Bronfman, 'an important part of the Nazi killing machine'. This campaign culminated on 27 April 1987 when President Kurt Waldheim of Austria was placed on the 'watch list' of persons denied entrance into the United States. This was certainly not a good example of American jurisprudence. Under the provisions of a law of dubious constitutionality, the head of a friendly nation was barred from the country on the basis of a secret report, without being granted a fair hearing or any other normal constitutional rights. No doubt future historians will judge harshly this action of the US government taken in response to pressure from an emotional American Jewish community.

On 28 April even the *Washington Post*, which supported the campaign against Waldheim, noted that the law barring the Austrian President from the US was 'partly flawed and arbitrary'. This is an understatement. Since entrance into the US is considered a privilege rather than a right, the US Justice Department holds that subjects of investigation for the 'watch list' are not entitled to know the charges against them or any of the other usual rights of constitutional due process. As a special favour Waldheim's American lawyers were sent a letter on 3 July 1986 which mentioned only broad areas of investigation without giving specific charges or mentioning the documentation against the Austrian President. Attorneys Tom Carraccio and Donald Santorelli were barred from the press conference on 27 April where the charges against Waldheim were revealed. Indeed, they were reduced to gathering essential information from the news media.[1] This disgraceful treatment of their president shocked the Austrian people.

The law under which Waldheim was barred from the US hinges on the word 'assisted', but what constitutes assistance in persecution has never been defined. One Justice Department official has commented that since Waldheim 'at the very least knew'[2] about criminal activity, he is eligible for inclusion on the 'watch list' of people suspected of assisting in persecution in the Second World War. But the press has given the impression that OSI has proved that Waldheim was involved in a wide range of criminal activity: all that has been shown is that, as a young staff officer, he had a general idea of what atrocities were being committed. Such 'evidence' would be thrown out of any court in the Western world. As we have seen, the Nuremberg Tribunal held that knowledge of war

1. Interviews with Tom Carriaccio and Donald Santorelli.
2. *Profil*, 18 May 1987.

crimes or being in the vicinity of where atrocities have been committed proves nothing. Clearly, if Waldheim can be put on the 'watch list', any veteran of the Wehrmacht could also be included. In effect the Justice Department had made service in the German armed forces in the Second World War a crime.

This completely destroys the previous distinction between people drafted into the German Army and members of Nazi criminal organizations. It represents a great victory for the SS veterans' associations who have argued for decades that service in the SS and Gestapo was no different from being an ordinary German soldier. Although the 'watch list' is secret, it is certain that almost all of those previously listed were members of Nazi criminal organizations.

If Waldheim is guilty then surely most Americans who served in Vietnam were guilty of having 'assisted in the persecution of persons' because of their Communist 'political opinion'. This would include many American veterans who are presently members of Congress as well as not a few officials of the Justice Department. By the OSI's logic, Lieutenant Colonel Oliver North, who is hailed as a hero by the Reagan administration, would be a major war criminal for his role in the anti-partisan warfare in Vietnam. By the generally accepted legal definitions North is not a war criminal – nor is Waldheim, who played a far less active role in military operations than North.

The OSI case against Waldheim is dubious on many other grounds. Most noticeable is that the Justice Department has ignored the evidence indicating that the UNWCC file on which the case against Waldheim is based was fabricated by the Soviets and Yugoslavs for political purposes. Statements by OSI imply that Waldheim was listed by the UNWCC because the charges in the dossier are genuine. But even Robert Herzstein, the former WJC consultant, recognizes that the *Odluka* was prepared for political purposes since the Yugoslavs wanted to embarrass Waldheim's superior, Austrian Foreign Minister Karl Gruber.[1] This has never been explained to the American public.

In its decision on the former UN Secretary General, the Justice Department has also ignored the ruling of the largely American court at Nuremberg that Yugoslav partisans were terrorists, in which case even if OSI had evidence to support many of its accusations against Waldheim, his actions would not be criminal. Waldheim has also been charged with crimes against Jews but the Israeli government made an official inquiry, which found no evidence to implicate Waldheim in the Holocaust.[2] If the Israelis have decided that Waldheim is not guilty of crimes against Jews, and an American court at Nuremberg has ruled that Yugoslav partisans were terrorists subject to the death penalty upon capture, what possible case can OSI make against an assistant adjutant who lacked any command powers?

Most disturbing of all is that in placing Waldheim on the 'watch list' OSI has so obviously violated its own criteria. As we have seen, Waldheim is considered to have 'assisted in persecution' because as an intelligence officer he must have had knowledge of atrocities. But in his book, former OSI director Alan Ryan states that no action should be taken against a suspect unless he 'personally took part or incited the persecution of which he is accused'.[3] Clearly OSI has not located a single document indicating that the former UN Secretary General incited or personally took part in persecution.

Ryan's defence of General Reinhard Gehlen, chief of all German intelligence operations in Russia and generally

1. *Profil*, 4 May 1987.
2. *Jerusalem Post*, 24 November 1986.
3. Alan Ryan, *Quiet Neighbors*, p. 248.

regarded as the best-informed Wehrmacht intelligence specialist of the Second World War, also causes concern. He defends the decision to bring Gehlen to the USA, since he '*never had anything to do with persecution*'[1] Ryan has repeatedly supported the decision to put Waldheim on the 'watch list' because of his knowledge of atrocities, but he believes General Gehlen, who knew a great deal more than Lieutenant Waldheim, did not meet the criteria for inclusion on the list despite detailed knowledge of the massacre of millions of Jews and other innocent civilians. Such a double standard is beyond comprehension. Ryan surely knows that, under the German system, a reserve lieutenant like Waldheim was hardly qualified to polish Gehlen's boots. Of course, there is a difference – Gehlen was not Secretary General of the UN when the anti-Zionist resolution was passed.

Ryan has a great deal to explain, including the fact that in 1980 OSI sent a member of its staff to the UN archives to inquire about the war crimes files just when I was about to publicize the fact that nothing had been done about these records for so long. Was OSI tipped off by the CIA, the State Department or the Israelis? Somewhat later Ryan told me that his office had the UNWCC list and was checking each name carefully. Did he discover Waldheim on the list? Did Eli Rosenbaum learn about Waldheim's name on the register while working for OSI in 1980 or in March 1986 as reported in the press? The present leadership of OSI has also to answer why Waldheim was placed on the 'watch list' based on a 'secret report'.

Despite this lack of evidence, it is not surprising that OSI would put Waldheim on the 'watch list'. The Office of Special Investigations faces considerable difficulty justifying its existence in a period of financial austerity. Originally

1. Ibid, p. 328.

founded in 1979 to make deportation cases against suspected war criminals who illegally entered the USA after the Second World War, it contemplates a dwindling pool of suspects, most of whom have died or are too old and feeble to face deportation hearings. The Waldheim case, however, has given OSI enough publicity to justify its existence for a few more years. It is a rule that any bureaucracy will always try to perpetuate itself. Certainly the powerful Zionist lobby in Washington had no reason to fear that OSI would resist the pressure to have Waldheim listed as a suspected war criminal. Thus it was a foregone conclusion that the former Secretary General would be placed on the 'watch list'.

Waldheim called the decision of the US Justice Department 'dismaying and incomprehensible', particularly in view of his long record of service to American interest dating back to 1945. In response to charges that he was responsible for shooting Yugoslav hostages, the Austrian President noted, in an apparent reference to the Iranian hostage crisis: 'I would like to point out in all modesty that in fact I was able to contribute to the freeing of those Americans who were held in Tehran.'[1]

The Justice Department's decision greatly accelerated the level of anti-American and anti-Semitic innuendo in the Austrian press. Placing President Waldheim on the 'watch list' without a fair hearing was certainly a legitimate grievance, but it is very disturbing to see Viennese journalists using phrases such as 'Jewish wire-pullers' and 'Jewish greediness'. It is certainly an exaggeration to call the treatment of Waldheim an 'inquisition' or to compare his ordeal to the passion of Jesus Christ. It is, however, hard to disagree with the statement about the World Jewish Congress in the Vienna tabloid *Neue Kronen Zeitung* on 16 May 1987: 'Edgar

---

1. *New York Times*, 29 April 1987.

Bronfman and his mephisto Israel Singer have made the esteemed organization founded by the European gentleman Nathan Goldmann into an American circus based on cheap sensationalism.'

Not surprisingly, Reagan has also become a popular subject of ridicule in the Austrian news media. Some of the comments ring true, such as the statement in the *Kurier* on 28 April: 'The Reagan administration has actually declared Austrian Federal President Kurt Waldheim an outlaw. This is a tremendous blow against friendly Austria. A catastrophe. The evidence is long overdue.' Few people in Austria would disagree with Austria's Foreign Minister who was quoted on 27 April by the press service of the Austrian People's Party as noting 'a campaign which is still being carried on by certain foreign groups against the head of state Dr Waldheim who has been elected by such a great majority'. Foreign Minister Alois Mock believed that the attacks on Waldheim had become 'a defamation campaign against our homeland. We must make every effort to oppose this.'

On 17 June 1987 the Austrian government officially demanded that Waldheim's name be removed from the Justice Department's 'watch list'. The Austrians rightly pointed out that 'the United States has produced no evidence to substantiate the allegations against Waldheim'. The Vienna government added, 'no country has the right to exercise jurisdiction over another nation's head of state'.[1] The Austrian protest had no effect since the small nation has no leverage in Washington to match the powerful Zionist lobby. However, the day after the protest Waldheim made it clear that he was not prepared to give up without a fight.

A spokesman for the Austrian President informed the press that Waldheim would meet the Pope in Rome on 25 June

1. *Washington Post*, 18 June 1987.

'with all the protocol of an official visit'.[1] The Austrian
Foreign Ministry called this planned meeting 'very gratifying'.
The Israeli government and its supporters had a field day in
the US press condemning the Pope for daring to defy their
ban on Waldheim. Prime Minister Yitzhak Shamir, who was
certainly knowledgeable about war crimes, called the Papal
visit 'a justification for the crimes of which Waldheim is
accused'. The president of the American Jewish Committee,
Theodore Ellinoff, characterized the planned meeting as
'morally and politically incomprehensible'. According to the
World Jewish Congress, Waldheim's visit to Rome was 'a
tragedy for the Vatican and a sad day for Catholic–Jewish
relations. This is the Pope who met with [PLO chairman]
Arafat. This is the Pope who refuses to recognize Israel.'
Most of the protests against the visit stressed the Vatican's
insensitivity to the Holocaust. 'Imagine how the millions who
died would feel if they knew that the Pope had received
Waldheim with full honours,' exclaimed Rabbi Marvin Heir,
dean of the Simon Wiesenthal Center.[2]

However, in a front page interview in the leading Italian
newspaper, but which was not reported in the American
press, Simon Wiesenthal took a different view. According to
the Nazi expert, no other Pope had done so much for the Jews
as Pope John Paul II. 'No other Pope has spoken so decisively
and unambiguously against National Socialism.'[3] In principle,
Wiesenthal did not oppose a Papal meeting with Waldheim,
but he felt it should have been held after a report was issued
by a committee of historians headed by Professor Hans
Rudolf Kurz of Switzerland, which planned to examine
Waldheim's Second World War military service. Wiesenthal
criticized the WJC for stirring up anti-Semitism in Austria by

1. *New York Times*, 18 June 1987.
2. *New York Times*, 26 June 1987.
3. *Corriere della Sera*, 23 June 1987.

making attacks not only against Waldheim but against the entire Austrian people. Wiesenthal expressed scepticism about the WJC charges, saying 'for accusations to be proved it is necessary to present documentation; so far this has not been done'.

Indeed, the total lack of any evidence to support the allegations against Waldheim was a key factor in the Pope's decision to receive the Austrian President. Buried in the back pages of the *New York Times* was the news that before the visit the Vatican had asked the US government to substantiate its charges against Waldheim, but 'the State Department refused to provide the Holy See with documentation relating to charges against Mr Waldheim'.[1] Since the Austrian President's accusers could not provide a single document against him, the Vatican cannot be reproached on legal or moral grounds for proceeding with the audience.

The American press gave a completely different slant to the story of Waldheim's Rome meeting. In the first paragraph of its front page story, the *New York Times* claimed that during Waldheim's Austrian presidential election campaign in the spring of 1986, 'documents were made public implicating him in the Nazi deportation of Greek Jews to death camps and in brutal reprisals against Yugoslav partisans'.[2] In reality, no documents implicating Waldheim in the deportation of Jews have ever been made public, and the only source suggesting that Waldheim was involved in reprisals consists of the totally discredited statements of the two German POWs contained in the bogus UNWCC dossier. Unfortunately, most of the US press coverage of the Waldheim visit was based on the erroneous assumption that there were documents implicating him in war crimes.

1. *New York Times*, 26 June 1987.
2. Ibid.

During the visit the Pope praised Waldheim as a man of peace and the freely elected President of Austria who had served two terms as Secretary General of the UN. The Pontiff also stressed the 'historical importance' of Austria to the Roman Catholic Church. Clearly Waldheim's position as President of one of the most staunchly Catholic countries in the world helps explain the Pope's willingness to receive the embattled former Secretary General. Despite the absence of evidence against Waldheim, the Vatican must have realized that the decision to receive him would result in Zionist protests. There are in fact other reasons, besides Austria's historic loyalty to the Catholic Church, which explain the Pontiff's decision to accept the consequences of a Waldheim visit.

Certainly there are many in the Vatican who have long had an antipathy to Zionism since it denies any Christian claim to the Holy Land. The Vatican Curia clearly wanted the world to know that, unlike the US government, the Church refused to do the bidding of the Zionists by participating in a smear campaign against a man whose war crimes exist only in the realm of fantasy. The more Waldheim is attacked by Israel and its agents in the United States, the more the Austrian President will be fêted in the Arab world and by Catholics who wish to antagonize the Zionist state. There is no basis for the idea that, as secretary general, Kurt Waldheim followed an anti-Israeli policy, but this myth is widely accepted. The Pope's reception of Waldheim had a salutary effect on the Church's image in the anti-Zionist Third World, which has helped to balance the Pope's recent conciliatory moves toward Israel.

On another level, the Pope must surely have taken into consideration Waldheim's strong support for Catholic political goals, including the Alpa-Adrica movement and the Slovenian and Croatian separatist movements in Yugoslavia.

Over the years Waldheim has built up credit with the Catholic Church. His persistent requests for an audience with the Pope were a way of saying that the Church owed him its support in his hour of need. Certainly Waldheim's playing of the Papal option is the first really intelligent move he has made since the WJC launched their campaign against him. The Pope's decision to have a second meeting with Waldheim in Vienna in June 1988 should further strengthen the Austrian President's popularity at home.

Waldheim's visit to the Pope in Rome in June 1987 touched off a wave of anti-Catholic rhetoric in the New York Jewish community which at times approached religious bigotry. Beginning with the Jewish leader who exclaimed 'The Pope has embraced Evil', the meeting was violently denounced. In an article in the *Jewish Press* on 3 July Julius Liebb charged that: 'In welcoming Waldheim, the Pope tried to cast the mantle of Church forgiveness over Nazi crimes.' Waldheim was described as the 'former United Nations Secretary General during whose term of office the scandalous "Zionism is racism" resolution was rammed through'. With regard to John Paul II, Liebb declared: 'We are not convinced by his protestations of brotherhood and compassion which without concrete follow-up translates into submission and loss of Jewish identity.' The Jewish journalist added: 'These sentiments are not to be interpreted as signifying that we are looking for a war with the Church. At the same time we should make it clear that neither will we accept the peace of spiritual death.'

Another article in the same edition by David Horowitz noted that Waldheim's Papal audience came a few days before Secretary General Javier Perez de Cuellar was scheduled to visit Vienna. Horowitz saw this as all part of an 'Unholy Trinity' between the PLO-dominated UN and the anti-Semitic Vatican uniting with neo-Nazis against the state of Israel and the Jewish people. Horowitz castigated the Pope for 'the nefarious deed of cleansing the suspect war criminal Kurt Waldheim with Holy Water'. Horowitz condemned Perez de Cuellar for 'the shameful exploitation of the UN for purposes of helping to orchestrate a "Save Waldheim campaign" which requires investigation. The behaviour of the Pope does not. Nothing that the Pope can do . . . will surprise the Jewish people except perhaps an *auto-da-fé* in St Peter's Square.'!

On 11 September 1987 the Pope met Jewish leaders in Miami to patch up the rift. But John Paul II did not satisfy many Jews. At the conclave the Pontiff mentioned the right of the Palestinians for self-determination. Earlier a reporter had asked him if he regretted the audience with Waldheim. 'No, it was necessary,' he replied. The Miami session set off another wave of anti-Catholic polemics. In the *New York Times*, Edgar Bronfman criticized the Jewish leaders who met John Paul II in Miami since the WJC president believed that an inter-faith dialogue must be based on 'Jewish dignity and Vatican substance'.

Because of his Polish background, John Paul II became the target of much of the resentment that had focused on Kurt Waldheim. In an article in the *Jewish Week* on 9 October 1987 Emmanuel Rackman wrote: 'This Pope deserves Jewish indifference even hostility' because 'he has demonstrated how well he was indoctrinated in his native land.' Many American Jews of Eastern European origin see the Polish Catholic clergy as a far more ancient enemy than the PLO or even the Nazis.

One of the most vicious anti-Catholic articles was published by Michael Lerner in the *Jewish Week* on 30 October 1987. According to Lerner, John Paul II had come to Miami 'to spit more directly into Jewish faces'. The Jewish journalist called the Pope 'a human autocrat acting as a God who is but flesh and blood'. John Paul II was criticized 'for hailing the world's highest-ranking former Nazi – Kurt Waldheim'. This should not be surprising because during the Second World War the Catholic Church 'helped play a major role in setting fire to the burning building of Europe'. Lerner obviously did not favour an inter-faith dialogue since he believed it was the role of the Jews 'to oppose through our deeds the many forms of *idolatry* that pervade the earth'. Other articles in the American Jewish press went further, even urging Jews to pray for the Pope's death. Clearly one of the most unfortunate results of the Waldheim affair has been this increase in religious bigotry among Austrians and American Jews.

In 1987 Kurt Waldheim issued his *White Book* which gives his interpretation of his career. A German language edition was published in Austria while an English language version was circulated for use by Austrian diplomats and the foreign press. But with the exception of an article in the *New York Post*, which called the report 'the Reich stuff', the American media largely ignored the 300-page explanation of Waldheim's career. There is in fact much important material in the *White Book*, but as usual Waldheim has badly blundered.

Instead of concentrating solely on refuting the Justice Department's false charges, the *White Book* attempts to support Waldheim's claims that he was not a member of the SA riding club and that he didn't know about the deportation of Jews. Thus his critics can point out Waldheim's absurd denials while ignoring his well-documented explanation of the serious charges against him. The *White Book* contains many of the same documents used by the WJC but gives a different, usually more accurate, interpretation. Waldheim's explanations, which are supported by numerous experts, are far more persuasive than the WJC report of 2 June 1986, which even a spokesman for the Israeli government considers amateurish.

Of particular interest in the *White Book* is Waldheim's claim that the *Odluka* was a phoney, prepared in 1947 by the Yugoslavs for political purposes but never used against him. The Austrian President denies the testimony of Kolendic and others that he was approached by the Soviets and Yugoslavs. It is amazing that both Waldheim and all his serious critics agree that the UNWCC file was prepared against him for political purposes but that this fact has almost never been mentioned to the American people.

It would appear that the Waldheim affair will be with us for some time. The World Jewish Congress are determined to make good their threat to keep up the pressure as long as Waldheim remains in office. The Austrian President shows no sign of resigning. His efforts to rally Catholic and Arab support make it clear that he is determined to last out his six-year term. It is difficult to see how this political struggle will turn out, but it should be clear that it has nothing to do with war crimes or the Holocaust. History will not be kind to Kurt Waldheim but it should be no more kind to his accusers.

CHAPTER VII

The Verdict

'Nazi files vanish – UN scandal' proclaimed the front page of the *New York Post* on 8 December 1987. So began the newspaper's most recent campaign against the world organization that is so unpopular in New York's Jewish community. The previous day Uri Dan, a reporter for the newspaper, had been the first journalist admitted to the previously secret portion of the UNWCC records. While reporters who were American citizens had to wait for permission from the US State Department in Washington, as an Israeli citizen Dan had been given immediate clearance from the Israeli UN Mission to use the newly declassified UNWCC files.

According to Dan, 'more than 400 previously sealed United Nations War Crimes Commission files have mysteriously vanished'. Dan worked closely with the Israeli UN mission in the preparation of his story. He quoted UN Ambassador Benjamin Netanyahu about the missing files: 'It means vital information concerning the greatest criminals in history have been destroyed.'

For more than a week the *Post* kept up its attack on the UN, announcing on its front page a 'Massive hunt for missing records'. Incredibly, this campaign against the UN was waged during the Reagan-Gorbachev summit, which was hardly mentioned in the *Post*! While journalists from the entire world converged on the historic signing of the missile disarmament treaty, the New York newspaper concentrated on its 'Shocking *Post* exposé of shameful UN scandal'. On 9 December, a *Post* editorial blamed UN archivist Alf Erlandson for misplacing the 'invaluable records', adding:

Some information on Waldheim was found in the file – information which inferentially links him to crimes.

But was more damning evidence destroyed? Data clearly is missing, and Waldheim certainly had the opportunity to remove it – to say nothing of the motive.

The suspicion that the UN archives were missing additional information on Waldheim was exaggerated into a certainty as the story was picked up by several New York radio stations and at least one TV station. Such irresponsible publicity can be understood only in the light of the hysteria existing in New York over Waldheim and the UN files. Gradually, however, the truth emerged.

On 14 December the *New York Times* reported that the case of the 'missing Nazi files' was a 'mystery that never was'. No information on Waldheim had ever been in the archives other than the three or four pages long since published. Of the 465 missing files, '441 were quickly found in a group of cases that had been adjourned, withdrawn, or involved war criminals who could not be identified'. Of the remaining twenty-four, some had been given dual numbers or had been returned to the member government. Eight files were still missing but there could be no question of any cover-up since these names were in the bound ledger containing all the cases delivered to the Commission. Removing a case could serve only to throw suspicion on someone, not cover him up.

At the beginning of his campaign over the UNWCC records in the spring of 1986, the Israeli ambassador had claimed that making the files available to researchers would 'open a whole new chapter in Holocaust research'. But as it became clear that the files really would be declassified, Netanyahu seemed to water down his earlier statements to the effect that opening the files might trigger revelations that would lead to the resignations of high officials in some countries. The ambassador told a Jewish newspaper, 'I haven't read the files. The opening of the files might have political consequences and it might not. We will know soon.' The list of names had been public information since May 1986 and the Israelis had obviously had the bound register for many years before that. If the list contained names of living West German and other Western officials, Netanyahu would never have pressed to make the files public. Why then had he led such a public campaign to open up the UN archives?

Of course, embarrassing the UN was a principal motive. But the Israeli Ambassador had more personal reasons as well. According to *Jewish World* the campaign over the UNWCC records 'can only rebound to Netanyahu's benefit as he leaves here next year to enter Israel's political wars'. Indeed, *Newsday* reported that 'some persons in the hunt for Nazis have complained privately that Netanyahu's domestic political ambitions have led him to exaggerate the importance of the files'. Another reason for the campaign was offered by Netanyahu himself: 'This is the model we should use now in our fight against the UN resolution of 1975 equating Zionism with racism.'

After the opening of the files a group of Israeli and American journalists entered the UN archives in an effort to substantiate Netanyahu's claims that they contained a huge amount of new information on the Holocaust. Privately, however, they conceded that they could find nothing to support Netanyahu's charges. Some of the journalists concentrated on a list of ten most wanted living Nazis recently prepared by the Simon Wiesenthal Center, but they did not realize that this list was not particularly reliable.[1]

---

1. Two of the ten were dead. Horst Shuman had died in Frankfurt in West Germany in 1985 (Robert Lifton, *Nazi Doctors*, p. 284). Heinrich Müller – 'It is accepted that he did not survive the War and if he did he did not survive for long.': Adalbert Rucberl, *N.S. Vernichtungslager im Spiegel deutscher Strafprozesse*, p. 246.

No information could be found to support Netanyahu's allegation that the British and Americans ignored evidence of the extermination of the Jews. An article on 26 December 1987, by Ralph Blumenthal of the *New York Times*, came close to the truth by noticing that the files 'shed new light on some of the Cold War tensions that split Eastern and Western members of the Commission, impeding efforts to prosecute some of the accused'. The cases cited by Blumenthal included Wilhelm Kopf who was accused of looting property in Poland but who later served as the British-appointed head of Hanover Province in occupied Germany. The Western Allies exerted pressure to have his name deleted from the list. The dismayed Poles were outvoted on the Commission and Kopf's name was removed. Political pressure was obviously used to both add and subtract names from the list.

Blumenthal also noted that the UNWCC records were considered by many scholars to be 'replete with inaccuracies and untested allegations'. He cited the example of Eugene Kogon, who is listed by the Commission for collaboration while serving as a prisoner at Buchenwald. But he is the author of *The Theory and Practice of Hell*, a classic work on concentration camps. His name on the list is obviously a 'tragic error', revealing that no one should be considered a war criminal simply because he is listed by the UNWCC. Indeed, when the former members of the War Crimes Commission agreed to open up the files they made the condition that all references to the files in books or articles specify that the information was not necessarily accurate.

Although some dossiers are extremely well researched, an examination of the files reveals that totally undocumented submissions were often given an 'A' rating. In one case (104/UK/It/2) involving the mistreatment of British prisoners at an Italian POW camp, the defendant was listed as 'the officer in command at and in the neighbourhood of

Bomba in Libya', without any suggestion of a name. This case was given an 'A' classification despite an entry in the file noting 'there is no evidence that there was a prisoner-of-war camp at Bomba'! In another case involving Yugoslavia against four Italians (587/Y/It/17), in which all the defendants were given an 'A' rating, the file states: 'It is to be assumed that until proof to the contrary is established, the accused acted on their own initiative ... It is not possible to forcsee at present any defence for the accused'. Most of the files, in fact, make it clear that the Commission acted on the basis of a presumption of guilt. There was thus no difficulty for Yugoslavia, or any other country, to get an 'A' classification for a totally bogus case prepared for the purpose of blackmail, which could be slipped in among a group of authentic cases.

There is a great deal of evidence in the newly opened files that makes it clear that Waldheim was listed for political reasons. As we have seen, the Belgrade National War Crimes Commission advised the Yugoslav embassy to give 'particular attention' to the Waldheim case. But on 19 February, the same day that Waldheim's *Odulka* was submitted to the UNWCC, the Yugoslavs also presented the file (7743/Y/G/556) of General Rudolf Leuters (who, it was later discovered, had died in Soviet captivity), a man described as 'Commander of all German forces in Croatia', and one of the highest Wehrmacht officers in the Balkans. It is impossible to imagine that, in 1948, the Yugoslavs would for purely legal reasons have given priority to a case against a reserve lieutenant such as Waldheim over that against General Leuters.

Waldheim was the only junior staff officer on the Yugoslav list submitted to the UNWCC. All the other suspects were either generals, combat officers who actually came in contact with their victims, or members of Nazi criminal organizations such as the Gestapo, SS, Secret Field Police, or Abwehr. The presence of several apparently genuine Abwehr

officers on the Yugoslav UNWCC list is what made
Waldheim's case seem real to the UNWCC staff, since he
was falsely described by the Yugoslavs as an Abwehr officer.
Many of the other UNWCC files are also false.

There is some interesting new information in the
UNWCC files on Italian war crimes, since so little has been
done on this subject, but there is nothing to sustain Ambassador Netanyahu's claim of massive new evidence on the
Holocaust. Historians will no doubt find much of interest in
the evidence that some of the UNWCC records were prepared for purposes of blackmail. For example, the recently
opened files reveal evidence to support the British claim that
the case against the former Bulgarian General Marinov was
'trumped up' (see p. 87). Marinov (3669/GR/B/1) had
commanded the 15th Bulgarian Division during the war.
The evidence against him included the statements of Greek
peasants who reported attacks by the 15th Bulgarian Division, but they did not implicate Marinov directly. Like
Waldheim, the main evidence against the Bulgarian Foreign
Minister consisted of the statements by POWs, including the
Bulgarian terrorist leader Anton Kaltev, and the Italian,
Lieutenant Giovanni Ravalli.

Kaltev had tortured and murdered thousands of Greek
civilians in disputed Macedonia. As the war criminal most
hated by the Greeks, it can be reasonably assumed that he
received less than considerate treatment, thus rendering any
statements signed by him somewhat suspect. In his trial for
his war crimes, Lieutenant Ravalli made a desperate effort
to save his life, including requests to various Greek and
British notables for a letter of reference verifying his
behaviour after Italy's capitulation in 1943. As in the
Waldheim case, no documents were presented to support
the statements of Kaltev and Ravalli against the Bulgarian
Foreign Minister. It would appear that British suspicions

about the Marinov case may be warranted.

The files also contradict some of the charges made against Waldheim, particularly with regard to Kozara. An article of 10 December 1987 in the German magazine *Stern* claims that documents from the Yugoslav archives prove that Waldheim was a war criminal because of his involvement in the selection of prisoners after the Kozara battle. The UNWCC records show that the commander of the West Bosnian Combat Group, General Fredrich Stahl, was charged by the Yugoslavs (7410/Y/G/482) for his role in the Kozara action. Waldheim has claimed that the selection of prisoners was delegated not to the quartermaster branch but to a separate panel. The Yugoslav UNWCC dossier against Stahl confirms this story since the Wehrmacht general is accused at the end of the Kozara action of 'setting up a special commission at Dubica with the tasks of singling out of the mass of interned prisoners, those who were alleged members of the NLA [partisans]. People sorted out in this way were shot.' There is no reason to believe that Waldheim was on this panel, indeed, none of the *Stern* documents or any documents from Kozara contains Waldheim's name.

Ironically, one extremely important document was published in *Stern* but its significance seems to have escaped even the author of the article. It is a 1952 Yugoslav memorandum (document 14) which lists Waldheim as a person not welcomed in the country because of his Wehrmacht service during the war. The document shatters Waldheim's claim that the Yugoslavs forgot about him after they listed him with the UNWCC in 1948.

It is extremely odd that the 1952 document mentions Warnstorff and Hammer of the Army Group E intelligence staff even though they were never listed in 1948. The 1952 Yugoslav document is clearly not evidence that Waldheim was a war criminal as implied by *Stern*, but is perhaps one more artefact in the Waldheim blackmail scheme – which did not end in 1948.

Early in 1988 the true facts of the Waldheim case became more apparent. On 22 January BBC Television broadcast an investigative news magazine story about the possible black-mail attempt against Waldheim. In the film I suggested that Waldheim's false war crimes file was known to the Ameri-cans, Soviets, Israelis and Yugoslavs. Former UN Under-Secretary General Brian Urquhart affirmed his belief that one branch of a government may not be informed by another agency of the same government, implying that the CIA and KGB may not have told the State Department and the Soviet Foreign Office about Waldheim's hidden past. This is hardly plausible since the very purpose of the intelligence services is to keep diplomats informed about such matters. If they did not already know about Waldheim's war crimes file in 1971 when he was a candidate for UN Secretary General, the Soviet and American diplomats would in any event have required a detailed report from their security agencies.

Even more unbelievable was the statement of Ray Cline, a frequent spokesman for the CIA, a man who in 1971 had been intelligence chief of the State Department. He sug-gested that with regard to war crimes information his superiors 'were sceptical of a good deal of the information of that period'. Cline added that the US government was not concerned about 'people who seemed to be getting along well'. Cline was clearly suggesting that the US government knew about Waldheim's Yugoslav war crimes file but approved him for Secretary General in 1971 because it was a fake. But surely the State Department realized that Waldheim could not have remained as Secretary General for forty-eight hours once it was revealed publicly that he was concealing his Balkan service in Hitler's army. Why did the US government support a man so susceptible to blackmail? The US, probably in co-operation with the USSR, obviously saw the war crimes file as an 'insurance policy' to prevent him from pursuing an independent policy as Secretary General.

During research for the BBC documentary Eli Rosenbaum, the former WJC legal counsel who claims to have found Waldheim's name in the National Archives, stated that while he worked for the Justice Department his office had received the UNWCC list but from 1980 to 1986 had never noticed Waldheim's name. This is clearly an impossible story. It takes only a few days for a trained investigator (of whom OSI has several) to make a thorough investigation of the register to see if it contains anyone prominent or unexpected. In 1986 it took me less than two days to go through the UNWCC register, where I found many unexpected German and Italian names. How is it possible that over a period of six years OSI missed the name of the UN Secretary General, particularly when his name was followed by a question mark and many rumours about his past were circulating in Washington? Besides, OSI director Alan Ryan told me in 1980 that his office was making a computer search of all the names on the list to see who had entered the USA. Waldheim's name would have showed up repeatedly since he frequently entered the country as a diplomat and in a private capacity.

In early February 1988 an international panel of historians was due to issue a report on Waldheim's military service. The anti-Waldheim group in Yugoslavia was therefore anxious to avert or discredit a not guilty verdict by the panel. On 1 February the West German magazine *Der Spiegel* published the text of a telegram which supposedly indicated that on 22 July 1942 Croatian Colonel Feodor Dragojlov notified his commanders: 'Most urgent Lieutenant Waldheim of General

Stahl's staff requests that the transport of 4,224 prisoners consisting mainly of women and children and around 159 old men is expected.' These people were purportedly being sent to concentration camps. If true, this document would be the first evidence that Waldheim committed a criminal act.

It soon became clear that the telegram was a fraud. Incredibly, *Der Spiegel* admitted paying $30,000 for a photocopy! Experts were able to establish, however, that the original had been typed on paper several decades old on a typewriter manufactured after 1949. It is not clear, however, if this was a recent forgery or a document manufactured by the Yugoslavs to blackmail Waldheim in the 1950s.

On 8 February, at the very last minute, this anti-Waldheim 'partisan clique' in Yugoslavia made a desperate effort to discredit the commission with a story claiming that Waldheim was the only German officer in a village where hostages were executed. This could, of course, be a serious matter except that the executions were carried out by Italians (*New York Times*, 8 February 1988). Once again, it was claimed that 'at the very least he knew'. But what could Waldheim do about atrocities committed by an army to which he did not belong? As we shall see, there is evidence that Waldheim did protest at atrocities committed by his own army.

When the report of the historical commission was delivered to the Austrian government, it was an anti-climax. It concluded that Waldheim knew about the atrocities but was not a war criminal. According to Israeli panel member Yehuda Wallach, Waldheim 'had been in no position to give orders as a lieutenant in the Balkans and so was not directly guilty'. Fellow commission member Manfred Messerschmidt agreed, telling the Bonn newspaper *Die Welt*: 'The accusation of participation in war crimes must therefore be taken as refuted.' On 10 February the *International Herald Tribune* reported that Hans Rudolf Kurz, head of the commission, had told Waldheim 'a documented criminal proceeding could not be carried out against him'.

A fuss developed, however, over the panel's removal of a passage in the report which declared Waldheim 'morally guilty' for his war-time service. This deletion was used by some of the news media to discredit the report but commission members indicated that they themselves had decided to make the change. As technical experts it is highly debatable that they were the appropriate body to make moral judgements.

The panel did criticize Waldheim for making efforts after the war 'to have his military past forgotten', but here lay the flaw since the commission had no mandate to investigate and explain to the public the real reason Waldheim concealed his past. Of course none of the nations involved, the USA, USSR, Israel, Yugoslavia or Britain, would have permitted an investigation of Waldheim's involvement with intelligence organizations since 1945.

Most of the headlines in the British and American press on the commission report proclaimed that 'Waldheim knew about war crimes'. This is true but hardly newsworthy. The end result is that after two years of investigation by several teams not a single document implicating him in war crimes has been discovered. It appears that the panel produced a negative report to avoid charges that they whitewashed Waldheim, and it is notable that the report contains no revelations about Waldheim's relations with their own national intelligence organizations.

In Britain there has been an effort to promote a campaign against Waldheim based on the young lieutenant's involvement with captured British commandos. The claim has been made that 'Soviet moles in the British intelligence service' had destroyed documents which incriminate Waldheim in the handing over of commandos to the SS for execution (*New*

York Times, 8 March 1988). Of course, there is no evidence for this assumption but as in so many other countries, lack of evidence has never hindered those determined to portray Waldheim as an 'accessory' in war crimes.

The section of the Kurz commission report dealing with British commandos was written by Gerald Fleming. Some in Austria have questioned whether the Anglo-Jewish historian was completely objective. Indeed, there are some omissions in the chapter by Fleming, who portrays British commandos as innocent victims of Nazi oppression. In reality the British commandos, who violated every rule of war and common decency, hardly deserved the protection of the Geneva Convention covering prisoners of war.

An objective expert on war crimes notes: 'The order issued to British sabotage troops was as brutal and primitive as anything the Nazis had dreamed up.'[1] British commandos were actually instructed 'Every soldier must be a potential gangster'! The standard equipment of British commandos included many instruments of torture used to extract information from captives who were eventually murdered since the commandos took no prisoners.

In his report Fleming cites no documents implicating Waldheim in the execution of the commandos but he criticizes him because the young lieutenant had knowledge of, and failed to prevent, the execution of the British terrorists. So far, the leader of the anti-Waldheim campaign in Britain, Robert Rhodes James,[2] has been unable to stir up the kind of anti-Waldheim hysteria such as exists in Italy where his

1. Eugene Davidson, *The Trial of Germans: Nuremberg 1946*, p. 388.
2. Rhodes James takes a rather simplistic view of the Waldheim case and is apparently unaware that all serious experts agree that the former Secretary General's UNWCC dossier has been fabricated for political purposes. On 18 February 1988 the Conservative MP told the *Standard* 'The Russians had one or two other things on their minds in 1946 than forging files.' The latest evidence (*The Times*, London, 31 March 1988) suggests that Waldheim may have been

knowledge of the deportation of Italian POWs has been used to discredit the former UN Secretary General.

The report notes that no instance could be found in which during the war Waldheim 'opposed an order to do something unjust'. But new evidence demonstrates that Waldheim *did* make an objection to atrocities. A *New York Times* story of 5 February 1988 notes that Professor Robert Herzstein, former WJC consultant, located a document of 25 May 1944 sent by Waldheim to his superiors:

The reprisal measures imposed in response to acts of sabotage and ambush have, despite their severity, failed to achieve any noteworthy success, since our own measures have been only transitory, so that the punished communities or territories soon have to be abandoned once more to the bands. On the contrary, exaggerated reprisal measures undertaken without a more precise examination of the objective situation have only caused embitterment and have been useful to the bands.

Herzstein conceeds that it was 'extraordinary for a junior officer to criticize Hitler's reprisal policy' but he tries to mitigate Waldhcim's courageous act since he maintains that it was made for 'practical rather than moral reasons'. But for those in Nazi Germany who opposed atrocities, criticism on practical grounds was risky enough; an objection made on moral grounds would have been nothing less than suicidal – and would have had even less chance of success.

In his classic study of Nazi Germany, Helmut Krausnick addressed the question of those rare individuals who objected to Nazi atrocities, noting that in a letter of protest it was necessary:

... to stick closely to the tactical line; the real humanitarian reason for opposition could not be allowed to appear nor could there be any hint of political criticism ... Since opposition has no official existence, it must hide behind some façade of agreement with the system. A blank refusal to conform – the real object – would be rejected out of hand; refusal is

---

covered up by the British government. This does not preclude the possibility of his involvement with Soviet and Yugoslav intelligence.

therefore expressed in the form of anxiety lest some instruction fail in its worthy object.[1]

For Waldheim it was particularly dangerous to criticize atrocities in view of his family's anti-Nazi record and his own tendency to speak out against the regime. It is not difficult to understand why, despite five years of service and a doctorate, he never rose above the rank of lieutenant. Certainly there is no reason to accuse the young Waldheim of 'moral guilt' for his military service. His behaviour under the Nazi regime was certainly morally superior to the tactics of the coalition of Zionists and 'the partisan clique' who have used forged documents and told numerous lies to embarrass Waldheim over the past two years. Indeed, Herzstein's book, *Waldheim: The Missing Years*, accentuates a major credibility problem for the World Jewish Congress since he contradicts the story that WJC legal counsel Eli Rosenbaum discovered Waldheim's name in the US National Archives. Herzstein claims that it was he, while working as a consultant for the WJC, and not the former Justice Department lawyer, who discovered Waldheim's name on the CROWCASS list in 1986. Herzstein offers as a witness John Mendelsohn, a National Archive employee who is now dead. Either Rosenbaum or Herzstein is not telling the truth or possibly neither party is correct. In any case, the American press, which has much publicized the discrepancies in Waldheim's story, has never mentioned the WJC's lack of credibility on the key question of how, and more important when, the organization learned about Waldheim's not-so-secret past.

Herzstein's claim to be objective in the Waldheim case is questionable. Clearly he has moved away from the extreme position taken by the WJC and agrees that Waldheim's UNWCC file was created for political purposes. But Herz-

1. Helmut Krausnick, *Anatomy of the SS State*, pp. 379, 376.

stein shows a definite tendency to accuse Waldheim on the basis of very thin evidence – or no evidence at all.

With regard to the extermination of the Jews, he claims that 'Waldheim served as an efficient cog in the machinery of Genocide' (p. 101). His only evidence is a report sent to Waldheim which has a sentence that in the town of Ionnia, 'the emerging Jewish committee there to be seen as a preparatory centre for the revolutionary movement'. There is no mention of a round-up or deportation of Jews in Ionnia nor is there any evidence that any action was taken on the basis of this one sentence – which Waldheim did not write. All that could be deduced from this sentence (assuming that Waldheim noticed it) is that the young staff officer knew that there were Jews in Greece who were suspected of having anti-German sympathies. There are no other documents sent or initialled by Waldheim that even mentioned the Jews. So Herzstein's claim that Waldheim played, 'a small but necessary role in the smooth execution of Hitler's Final Solution', is clearly unsupportable.

Herzstein also claims that 'Waldheim had been involved in the notorious Kozara deportations' ((p. 205). But the Kurz commission report notes that with regard to Kozara, 'a concrete indication of Waldheim's exact involvement in questions of transport and problems of camps has not become known'. None of the documents published by Dusko Doder in the *Washington Post* or the 'evidence' in *Stern* makes a case against Waldheim for Kozara. In fact, Herzstein, like everyone else, fails to publish a single document on the deportations from Kozara which has Waldheim's name on it. He suggests that the Americans covered up the Croatian war criminal, Oscar Turina, because he had incriminating evidence about Waldheim's role at Kozara. But this argument is unimpressive since Herzstein does not cite any documents, witnesses or other evidence which links Waldheim to Turina. The Ameri-

can historian simply assumes that the reserve second lieutenant who worked in the supply section must have been a
person of importance at Kozara because he received the
worthless medal during this period.

Herzstein admits that Waldheim 'was not a war criminal
himself' but he calls him a 'facilitator' who belongs on the
Justice Department 'watch list' because 'the documentary
evidence against him was conclusive'. But articles in the
Austrian magazine *Profil* published in the spring of 1987
contained copies of the Justice Department documentation
on Waldheim which make it clear that OSI has not a single
piece of paper which proves anything that is remotely 'conclusive'. Indeed, on 18 February 1988, the *New York Times* noted
that the OSI's 'secret report' contained forty-nine pages on
the deportations, none of which even had Waldheim's name
on them. The claim that 'they had no doubts he would have
had to be involved' does not inspire confidence in the Justice
Department's case against Waldheim.

In view of its lack of evidence against Waldheim, it is not
surprising that the Justice Department refused to co-operate
with the Vienna Commission. In a letter (*New York Times*, 5
Dec 1987) to General James Lawton Collins, the American
member of the panel, OSI declined to provide documentation
on Waldheim but defended its decision to place him on the
'watch list', claiming:

It has been suggested that the US action resulted from the fact that Kurt
Waldheim was in the area where crimes and acts of persecution took
place and that mere proximity to such activities warranted a watch list
decision. That simply is not the case and we have never so represented.

On the contrary, the findings are that that there is sufficient evidence
to implicate Mr Waldheim personally . . .

This letter strongly suggests that OSI had placed
Waldheim on the 'watch list' because it had definite proof
that he was involved in atrocities, not just knowledge of war

crimes. According to the *New York Times*, 'a critical body of documentation remains locked away in the United States Justice Department's Office of Special Investigations'. Indeed the Justice Department has long claimed to have solid documentation which proved Waldheim's guilt.

The man who made the decision to place Waldheim on the 'watch list' was Attorney-General Edwin Meese. Early in 1988 he had the dubious distinction of being under simultaneous investigation in relation to possibly more scandals than any other cabinet member in US history – mainly for indiscretions involving his close ties to the Zionist lobby, including a scheme to bribe Israeli officials. Meese was also the man who decided that OSI would not co-operate with the Kurz commission. But after the panel's report the Justice Department took a different line stating that the panel's 'report which found that Mr Waldheim must have been aware of atrocities and did nothing to stop them supported the Justice Department's decision last year to place Mr Waldheim on the watch list'.

Does knowledge of war crimes and failure to attempt to stop them constitute 'assistance in persecution'? Alan Ryan, former director of OSI, believed that General Gehlen, the head of all German intelligence on the Eastern front, did not assist in persecution. General Gehlen had infinitely more knowledge of and opportunity to block persecution than Lieutenant Waldheim. Clearly the Justice Department shares the 'moral guilt' of the 'partisan clique' in Yugoslavia and the American Zionist lobby who have carried on the campaign against Waldheim.

General Gehlen, who freely entered the USA and had close ties to the US military, was not the only man in a conspicuous position to have a record far worse than Waldheim, yet one that was overlooked by the same people who are so outraged at the latter's ambivalent military service.

In 1965 Alexander Toeroek was appointed as embassy councillor and chargé d'affaires at the German embassy in Tel Aviv. Toeroek was an ethnic German born in Hungary. In 1944 he had been an official at the Hungarian embassy in Berlin at a time when 400,000 Jews were deported from Hungary to Auschwitz and gassed. As legation secretary he was possibly involved in the deportations, since 'the Hungarian Mission in Berlin may well have been a place for receiving or forwarding Nazi orders including those concerning the annihilation of Hungarian Jewry'.[1] Of Toeroek we can certainly say 'at the very least he knew' about the extermination of hundreds of thousands of innocent civilians. An examination of German and Hungarian documents might prove Toeroek's direct participation in the Holocaust. But no such investigation was begun since the Israeli government did not wish to embarrass West Germany, which was supplying important financial and diplomatic support to the Zionist regime. There has clearly been a great deal of selective indignation with regard to Waldheim, a man whose war record has never been put in its proper perspective.

When evaluating Waldheim's military career several factors should be kept in mind. War is essentially a dirty, ugly business. Serious war crimes investigations take into account that many activities that would be criminal in peace are routine procedure in a military conflict. To any specialist on the Second World War, Kurt Waldheim's record seems rather ordinary and benign, but when described out of context it can be made to seem criminal to people unfamiliar with the nature of war.

The conflict in Yugoslavia was particularly brutal. The press has portrayed Tito's partisans as valiant freedom fighters. In reality they slaughtered not only defenceless German

---

1. Inge Deutscheron, *Berlin and Jerusalem*, p. 338.

POWs but hundreds of thousands of innocent Yugoslav political opponents. Of course Hitler's attack on Yugoslavia in 1941 was a 'crime against peace'. After the war General Löhr was hanged by the Yugoslavs for his order to bomb Belgrade in 1941 – not for any actions taken as commander of Army Group E. Kurt Waldheim did not serve in Yugoslavia until 1942, thus press reports which attempt to link him to Löhr's conviction as a war criminal are misleading.

There can be no question that Army Group E committed enormous atrocities. But there is no reason to label all 500,000 men who served in it as war criminals, any more than the half million Americans who served in Vietnam. Some would say that all who served in Army Group E or Vietnam are 'accessories' or 'morally guilty', but if all are guilty then none are guilty. Over the years specific criteria have been established as to who is a war criminal; the case against Kurt Waldheim does not meet those criteria.

When the Waldheim affair first became public in the spring of 1986, I supported the efforts of the World Jewish Congress. Like most people, I did not think they would make such a blizzard of accusations unless they had some evidence against the former Secretary General. It seemed logical to assume that with so much smoke there had to be some fire. However, after two years of my own research it is clear that Kurt Waldheim is guilty of many things – but being a war criminal is not one of them. Some of the statements made by Waldheim's critics are ludicrous. There has been an effort to turn him into a demon. This is clear from some of the remarks by Austrian playwright Peter Handke, who calls Waldheim 'the ghost from Transylvania' who put the 'mark of Dracula on the sleeping body of the people'.[1] Such extremist rhetoric has gained much sympathy for

1. Rosenzweig and Cohen, *Waldheim*, p. 177.

Waldheim in Austria and helped keep him in office.

The former Secretary General's service in Yugoslavia was not demonic. The Waldheim affair is not a war crimes case but essentially a story of blackmail and international intrigue. However, since it was the WJC which broke the Waldheim story on the international scene, it was they who set an agenda focusing on Waldheim's military record rather than his involvement in the political intrigue of post-war Vienna.

Waldheim hid his past not because he was a war criminal but because he feared the revelation of the fake war crimes file. On 5 November 1945, when he filed his application for the Austrian Foreign Office, he mentioned both his membership in the SA cavalry club and his service in Yugoslavia. With such a record, Waldheim could have been an Austrian official but not Secretary General of the UN. Of course the young Waldheim had no way of knowing in 1945 that he would some day be a candidate for that position. After 1948, when Waldheim may have been threatened with the war crimes file, he concealed not only his service in Yugoslavia but also his Nazi student affiliations, the revelation of which could have triggered an investigation which would in turn lead to the fake file.

That the file was prepared for political purposes is accepted by Waldheim and all serious researchers on this subject. He claims, however, that the file was never used by the Yugoslavs or Soviets. This seems unlikely in view of the testimony of the many witnesses in Yugoslavia who have defied their government's displeasure by speaking honestly on this subject. As well as the Soviets and the Yugoslavs, it is quite possible that the Americans, the British and eventually the Israelis knew about the file and used it to their advantage. Waldheim was involved in an elaborate web of intrigue, the details of which we probably will never know. It *is* unlikely that he favoured the Soviets, as charged by many of his critics.

Ironically it is for his involvement in post-war political intrigue, not his military service, that Kurt Waldheim is 'morally guilty'. In particular he must be condemned for accepting the position of UN Secretary General while concealing his tour of duty in the Balkans. Even if his hidden past was not used by any nation to influence him, as Waldheim claims, he showed an extreme lack of concern for the good name of the UN by accepting the office of its chief executive despite his vulnerable position. Waldheim surely realized that the exposure of his hidden past would damage not only him but the organization he swore to serve. He showed equal disregard for the good name of the Austria he professes to love by engaging in a campaign for the presidency even after it became clear that he was an embarrassment to his country.

But blame must be shared by the countries who cynically elected Waldheim as UN Secretary General, demonstrating a gross disregard for the organization and the principles on which it was founded.

Sources

Unpublished documents
Public Record Office – British diplomatic correspondence
United Nations Archives – UNWCC files and the Secretariat's Central
Registry of correspondence
United States National Archives – captured German and Italian military
records
Washington National Record Center – American diplomatic
correspondence
Over the years I have collected various unpublished documents from a
variety of sources. These include copies of letters, classified government
documents and transcripts. I have cited these where possible in the text.

Personal interviews
Since 1979 I have spoken to a wide variety of people involved in the
story of Kurt Waldheim and the UN war crimes files. In most cases I
have made direct quotations from transcripts written during or
immediately after the interview. As noted in the text the names of
several Yugoslav interviewees have been kept confidential.

Investigation reports
Most reports on Waldheim are not available to the public. The reports
of the WJC and the Kurz Commission have been made available to
scholars and journalists. Waldheim's *White Book* has been published in
German in Austria. The US Justice Department's report is still secret
but most of the documentation is known to students of the Waldheim
case. Unfortunately all of these reports deal exclusively with Waldheim's
war service while avoiding the far more important question of his
post-war involvement with intelligence organizations.

Books
Abernathy, M. D., Delys, M., & Williams, Phil, *The Carter Years*,
    London, Frances Pinter, 1984
Bader, William B., *Austria Between East and West 1945–1955*, Stanford,
    Stanford Press, 1966

Bailey, Sidney, *The Procedure of the UN Secretary Council*, Oxford, Clarendon Press, 1975

Bamford, James, *The Puzzle Palace*, Boston, Houghton, Mifflin, 1982

Barron, John, *KGB: The Secret Work of Soviet Secret Agents*, London, Corgi Books, 1975

Bower, Tom, *The Pledge Betrayed*, Garden City, N.Y., Doubleday, 1982

Davidson, Eugene, *The Trial of Germans: Nuremberg 1946*, New York, Macmillan, 1966

Deutschron, Inge, *Berlin and Jerusalem: The Strange Coalition*, New York, Macmillan, 1972

Findley, Paul, *They Dare to Speak Out*, Westport, CT, Lawrence Hill & Co., 1985

Franck, Thomas M., *Nation Against Nation*, New York, Oxford University Press, 1985

Grunberger, Richard, *The 12-Year Reich*, New York, Holt Rinehart & Winston, 1971

Herzstein, Robert E., *Waldheim: The Missing Years*, New York, Arbor House, 1988

History of the United Nations War Crimes Commission, London, Hutchinson, 1949

Kahn, David, *Hitler's Spies: German Military Intelligence in World War II*, New York, Collier Books, 1978

Kaufmann, Johan, *United Nations Decision Making*, Rockville, MD, Sijthoff & Noordhoof, 1980

Khol, A. (ed.) *Die Kampagne: Waldheim Opfer oder Täter?*, Munich, Herbig Verlag, 1987

Koch, H. W., *The Hitler Youth*, New York, Stein & Day, 1976

Lauriere, Herve, *Assassin au Nom de Dieu*, Paris, La Vigie, 1951

Lifton, Robert, *Nazi Doctors*, New York, Basic Books, 1986

Lucas, James, *Last Days of the Third Reich*, New York, Morrow, 1986

Martin, David C., *Wilderness of Mirrors*, New York, Ballantine, 1980

Molden, Otto, *Der Ruf des Gewissen – Der Österrichischen Freiheitskampf*, Vienna, Harold Verlag, 1958

Moynihan, Daniel Patrick, *A Dangerous Place*, Boston, Little, Brown, 1978

Murphy, Brendan, *The Butcher of Lyon*, New York, Empire Books, 1983

Posner, Gerald and Ware, John, *Mengele: The Complete Story*, New York, McGraw Hill, 1986

Ranelagh, John, *The Agency: The Rise and Fall of the CIA*, New York, Simon & Schuster, 1986

Robach, Livia, *Israel's Sacred Terrorism*, Belmont, MA, AAUG Press, 1980

Rosenzweig, Luc and Cohen, Bernard, *Waldheim*, New York, Adana Books, 1987

Rubenstein, Alvin Z., *Yugoslavia and the Non-Aligned Movement*, Princeton, NJ, Princeton University Press, 1970

Ruckerl, Adalbert, *N.S.-Vernichtungslager*, Munich, Deutscher Taschenbuch Verlag, 1977

Ryan, Allan, *Quiet Neighbors*, New York, Harcourt, Brace Jovanovich, 1984

Saidel, Rocelle, *The Outraged Conscience*, New York State University Press, 1986

Schlesinger, Arthur, *Robert Kennedy and His Times*, Boston, Houghton, Mifflin, 1978

Schlesinger, Thomas O., *Austrian Neutrality in Postwar Europe*, Vienna, Wilhelm Braumuller, 1972

Schoenbaum, David, *Hitler's Social Revolution*, New York, Doubleday, 1966

Seidman, Hillel, *United Nations: Perfidy and Perversion*, New York, M.P. Press, 1982

Shevchenko, Arkady N., *Breaking With Moscow*, New York, Ballantine, 1985

Sick, Gary, *All Fall Down*, New York, Random House, 1985

Stoessinger, John G., *The United Nations and the Superpowers*, New York, Random House, 1977

Urquhart, Brian, *A Life in Peace and War*, New York, Harper and Row, 1987

Waldheim, Kurt, *The Austrian Example*, New York, Macmillan, 1973

Waldheim, Kurt, *The Challenge of Peace*, New York, Rawson Wade, 1980

Waldheim, Kurt, *In the Eye of the Storm*, New York, Alder & Adler, 1985

Wiesenthal, Simon, *Murderers Among Us*, New York, McGraw Hill, 1967

Index